# FAITHFUL
# HEARTS

# FAITHFUL HEARTS

## The Adventure of Spiritual Mentoring

### JAN KEMPE

**Discovery House Publishers**

*Books, music, and videos that feed the soul with the Word of God*

Box 3566 Grand Rapids, MI 49501

Discovery House Publishers is affiliated with RBC Ministries, Grand Rapids, Michigan.

Discovery House books are distributed to the trade exclusively by Barbour Publishing, Inc., Uhrichsville, Ohio.

Unless otherwise indicated, Scripture references are from the New International Version (NIV), © 1973, 1978, 1984 by the International Bible Society. Used by permission of Zondervan Bible Publishers.

**Library of Congress Cataloging-in-Publication**

Kempe, Janice.
Faithful hearts : the adventure of spiritual mentoring / Jan Kempe.
p. cm.
ISBN 1-57293-128-0
1. Spiritual formation. I. Title.
BV4511.K36  2005
253.5—dc22

2005005359

Printed in the United States of America

05 06 07 08 09 /CHG / 10 9 8 7 6 5 4 3 2 1

To Jon,
my love,
still my very best friend.
Not many are blessed to find what we have.

And to Krista, Kevin, and Mike,
who are loyal, kind, and loving people,
who walk in integrity,
whose company I enjoy,
and of whom I am very proud.
You're just what I always wanted.

# CONTENTS

*"All authority in heaven and on earth has been given to me. Therefore go and make disciples of all nations, baptizing them in the name of the Father and of the Son and of the Holy Spirit, and teaching them to obey everything I have commanded you. And surely I am with you always, to the very end of the age."*

*Jesus, as recorded in Matthew 28:18–20*

*Introduction*

# LESSONS FROM
# A BROWN DUCK

"GOD, WHAT DO you want from me?" A change in circumstances, an unforeseen turn of events, had left me confused about the direction of my life and ministry. My time in the Word was not helping me understand what my next steps should be, and the silence of listening in prayer was about to drive me nuts. "Please, Lord, what do you want from me?"

The opportunity to go for a walk with a friend was a welcome distraction. As we passed a pond I noticed a female duck swimming with nine ducklings. The ducklings were still a bit yellow and fuzzy, but the first signs of brown feathers were changing them from cute to drab. We stopped to watch for a moment, but my friend had a schedule to keep, so we walked on and left the ducks behind. However, I did wonder if any of them would survive these turtle-infested waters.

Today I was walking the same route with my dogs . . . once again escaping the same perplexing questions and the same confusing silence. As I approached the pond, I noticed a drake and a hen swimming rapidly away from the shore. Between them bobbed a wave pool of tiny brown heads, now bearing only a slight trace of the yellow feathers that had been in their coats last week. I stopped to count the ducklings . . . seven in all. "It seems you have lost two of your babies," I said aloud. "I'm glad to see there are two of you watching the ones you have left, but when the turtles snap from underneath, I'm sure more ducklings will vanish. I'm sorry for your loss. Life can be tough."

(This is why I choose to walk mostly with dogs. They don't mind in the least when I stop to share my wisdom or offer my greetings to non-human beings.)

As I finished my impromptu duck blessing (not actually something I learned in seminary), a flurry of little webbed propellers churned up a wake behind the departing family. It was a dawdling duckling that obviously hadn't been listening when his parents said, "Let's go. *Now*, please." He neared the family about the same time that a second beautiful, green-headed drake flew in and landed on his outstretched webbed feet very close to the group. As he swam over to the family, I wondered who belonged to whom, and how this mature threesome would get along. Not being familiar with the dynamics of duck relationships, I was intrigued enough to linger and watch.

Suddenly, mother duck turned her back and left her young in the care of the males who seemed to be guarding the boundaries for the floating mass of ducklings. She paddled quickly toward the shore, close to where I stood, and my eye caught a frenzied brown commotion that had escaped my notice before. She swam right up to the place where the water stirred and then abruptly turned and began swimming back in the direction of her brood. Out of the grassy shallows emerged a seemingly endless, single-file line of ducklings. I counted as they set off . . . one, two, three . . . five, six, seven . . . ten, twelve . . . hold on here . . . fifteen babies were following her back to the two mallards and the original eight.

"Twenty-three ducklings? Is that even possible?" I wondered aloud. "This is really odd," I informed my dogs.

We suspended our walk while I waited for a new development in the unfolding duck drama, but they only bobbed and floated peacefully about twenty feet away from the shore—mama duck, two gorgeous drakes, and twenty-three babies.

There had to be another mother duck somewhere! A clutch of duck eggs is nine to eleven. Twenty-three eggs just couldn't fit in that tiny duck mama, could they? But there were no other mothers to be seen.

Perhaps there was an extremely large, satisfied turtle sleeping off his feast at the bottom of the pond. Maybe a dog or a cat had surprised her in the shallows, or maybe it was just her day to run off and "find herself." I don't know, and that's not the direction my mind wandered during the whole duck encounter.

What overwhelmed me as I wept over the little drama was the reality of the lesson before me. Generations of the duck family had seen a need to nurture and protect their progeny, and occasionally take in some who, for some unknown reason, found themselves alone. Their purpose, which seemed to be clearly understood by the three adult ducks, was simply to come alongside . . . it's the way God designed them. Refusing would leave fifteen ducklings alone and vulnerable in dangerous turtle-infested shallows.

I'm not at all sure how a duck parent goes about teaching a duckling to be a duck. I know about imprinting, that strange phenomenon that causes a newly hatched bird to identify and emulate the first living being it encounters. But I'm not at all sure how ducks can even recognize the group to which they belong (give me ten female ducks and I see replicas, not individuals); yet when families of ducks share the same pond, those babies seem to know which mama to follow. How does a duck learn to fly when floating seems sufficient to get him where he needs to go, and when he has no nest in a tree from which to launch? And don't even get me started on the way they fly in a V, at appropriate times, to faraway places . . . and then find their way back in the spring! The complexity of it all boggles my mind. But the need for the young to tag along with the grown . . . that is something I understand.

Now, I am a reasonably intelligent person, with more than an average education, and yet a mass of wiggly feathers has undone me this day. I know that all nature is created to reveal the character, the plan, and the power of God to those who will notice. "For since the creation of the world God's invisible qualities—his eternal power and divine nature—have been clearly seen, being understood from what has been made, so that men are without excuse" (Romans 1:20). Today creation is screaming at me . . . "This is my design! Some are called to lead, some to follow, but what I want most from you is just to come alongside. Now that you've seen this, you have no excuse."

And so my walk ended and I returned home to the comfort of my office, to contemplate the purpose of my ministry. The light on the phone blinks, alerting me that someone has left a message. My calendar bears names and times and meeting places, and the inbox of my e-mail is full of messages. I face my day with the knowledge that I am doing exactly what God designed me to do. The calling to intercede, to be a companion and a mentor, is the highest calling I can imagine. Once again tears come as the meaning of this honor sinks into my heart.

Today things make sense. My question has been answered. I know that the God who created me has the plan, the job description, and the resources I need. I am called to serve as a plain brown duck with *way* more ducklings than is reasonable. It's what I do. It's God's design for me. I come alongside. Today I understand that to disregard this sacred calling would leave some of His beloved children bobbing alone in unfriendly waters.

> O God, Creator of every living thing, keep my eyes open to see the way you care for your creation. Give me a willing heart that is content to accomplish simple acts of faithfulness and to minister with a love that may never be noticed by anyone but you. Open my eyes to any hatchlings that cannot begin to navigate the waters of their lives alone and show me how to come alongside. This is discipleship. This is what you have commissioned your followers to do. Sanctify the experiences of my life by using them to teach the next generation what they need to know about your faithfulness, and as I come alongside them, may they notice only you. Amen.

# Chapter One

# IT'S ALL ABOUT
# THE WALK

HAVE YOU EVER met someone who reminds you of Jesus? When that person speaks, you feel compelled to listen. When you need counsel and comfort, that person's face comes to mind. When life throws you a curve and you have no simple answers to complex problems, that person is there to help you seek the answers you need. And when answers can't be found, that person is there to assure you that it might not be the answers that will ultimately solve your problem anyway, but rather the presence of God in your confusion. When you encounter a person like this, someone who is consistently surrounded with a sense of peace and an excitement about the sufficiency of God in any situation, chances are you are in the company of a disciple of Jesus.

How does one become a disciple of Jesus? By walking with Him everyday. Let me explain.

A healthy walk with Christ results in certain character traits that the apostle Paul referred to as the fruit of the Spirit: "love, joy, peace, patience, kindness, goodness, faithfulness, gentleness and self-control" (Galatians 5:22–23). These are the things you have probably noticed in the person we just described. But just how does a person come to have this healthy walk? There is no quick and easy way to spiritual maturity. Trying to build these desirable characteristics into your own life is not something to be accomplished by willpower or through an eight-week study. The key to being a patient person, for example, is not to wake up in the morning fully determined to be patient. These characteristics of Jesus only flourish in a life that is controlled by the Holy Spirit (hence the term "fruit of the Spirit"), and are natural developments that occur as a person walks with God. In other words, these characteristics don't flourish in our life because we focus on the fruit, but rather when we learn to keep our focus on God. As we walk with Him, we become something new, something we are unable to become on our own.

When Jesus had been ministering for a few years and had gotten people's attention with His amazing teaching and His extraordinary, unflappable presence, He tried to explain that His reason for coming was to enable people to expect and to live just such extraordinary lives. In the tenth chapter of John, we see Jesus trying to communicate to the religious authorities of His day the good news that He had come to bring forgiveness of sins and a new way of life. Because of this good news, they no longer needed to be bound to a law that burdened them. As Jesus sought to help them understand His purpose, He said, "'The thief comes only to steal and kill and destroy; *I have come that they may have life, and have it to the full*'" (John 10:10, emphasis added).

Full life! The reason for this book is to encourage believers to understand that not only is this possible for us, but it is also ultimately what our hearts desire and is the only thing that will satisfy us and bring us peace. More than that, it is an insult to God when we settle for anything less than this life to the full. In the words of our present culture of extreme games, extreme challenges, and extreme makeovers: God offers us extreme life through Jesus Christ! When the fruit of the Spirit is evident in our lives, it is a symptom that conditions are right for extreme life.

Life to the full—at least as I understand it—means that I am living the life God intended when He created me. I imagine Him watching, encouraging, and enabling me, totally involved in my progress and my regress; forgiving and bidding me to take my next step. The message of Scripture has often been portrayed as that of an angry God, pointing His finger at sinful creatures and holding out a list of rules. A more truthful picture is one of a loving God who extends His hand, palm up, fingers curling inward, beckoning His beloved to take one more step . . . come a little further . . . don't give up.

As we progress through this book together, it is my intention to give you glimpses of life to the full and to impress upon you that God desires nothing less for you. It is also my intention to entice you, as you learn to walk with God, to turn around and extend encouragement to those following after you. There isn't one of us who cannot be equipped to mentor someone else or to pass on the same encouragement that brought us to know Jesus.

Because people come to an understanding of God at different ages and through different circumstances, I would like to share with you a snapshot of how my walk began. None of us comes to faith alone. Jesus extended a personal invitation to certain men and women to walk with Him.

19

One of them extended that invitation to someone else, who in turn extended it to someone else . . . down through the convulsive pages of human history, one person at a time, until the invitation eventually reached my grandparents. They passed it along to my parents, who offered it to me. Each connection involved telling the story and extending the invitation to join in this wonderful and very personal chain of witnesses. Now, I have the awesome responsibility of extending that hand to the people in my life.

Picture it! A very real chain of hands, connecting you to the nail-scarred hands of the Savior. As you picture this, consider two things: Who is responsible for helping you in your walk with God, and how can you turn around and help someone else?

## My Walk

My walk had a privileged beginning. I accepted Jesus into my heart at the age of four or five. My mom said so. I don't remember my first encounter with Jesus, but then I don't remember my first encounter with my mother either, and I've never questioned that relationship. I figure my first encounter with both must have been in the delivery room, because the Jesus I have come to know would never let my mother go through something like that alone. And so I had an early start as a child of God, a follower of Jesus.

Growing up in a home where Jesus' name was spoken with respect and love . . . and often . . . is probably my most valuable inheritance. My parents didn't speak about Him like some remote being or mystical power that resides in church. He wasn't some far-removed source of guilt that required obedience to a list of rules. No, Jesus was as real a part of my family as any of the rest of us.

20

My dad was an intelligent man who taught science to physically challenged high school students. My mom served as a lunch lady to the younger students. I watched and listened as they told stories of these remarkable children, completely aware that my parents loved the people they served—sometimes, it seemed, as much as they loved me. And for some reason, that was okay.

Each summer of my youth our family moved up to a beautiful lake to live and work at Portage Lake Covenant Bible Camp. Mama would cook, my sisters would cook, my brother was lifeguard, and his wife was the nurse. For many years I was too young to do anything other than explore the tops of trees and the bottom of the lake. My dad did most everything else that needed to be done around the camp, and many of my days were spent "working" alongside him. He had me paint the log cabins with a brush and a bucket of water to make the red paint shine, so that things looked fresh and special for the campers as they arrived. He had me move piles of bricks and dig holes and find worms for the fishermen. Each job was uniquely important, and I earned top dollar—or maybe I should say top quarter—for my efforts. But the best thing my dad did was stop occasionally and make me look and listen.

"Do you hear that bird?" he would say. "What do you suppose he looks like?" We would look until we found the answer, and little by little I learned about life in the fields and at the beach. We discovered large green moths the size of my hand and little, pink, newborn mice, fish with huge mouths, and lovely blue snakes. Each creature had a name and some distinguishing characteristic that made it different from every other creature. Some I could touch and some (like the wonderful assortment of skunks!) were best left alone.

21

I remember Dad waking me up early one morning and taking me down to the beach. He had a coffee can, some matches, a spoon, two eggs, and several strips of bacon. "How could we make breakfast?" he asked. Then he watched patiently as I gathered sticks for the fire. He watched as I lit the fire and put the can over the top of it, and he watched as the fire went out. I learned that morning that fire needs oxygen, and after we cut a few vents in the can he watched as I arranged the bacon on the can, tipped the fat off, and added the eggs. He watched as I guarded the precious meal from the blowing sand. My father loved me enough to let me learn things by trying. More than that, he loved me enough to lead me to places where I would want to learn. And he loved me enough to eat his sandy bacon and crunchy egg and pronounce it the "best breakfast I have ever had!"

I could ask my dad any question I couldn't find an answer to myself. More often than not he would answer with another question that would make me think and struggle to find my own answer. He spent time with me— lots and lots of time. He told me stories and we laughed. I saw how he adored my mom. I watched as he prayed before every meal, usually a tear or two slipping in with his thanks. We sang in the car and sometimes whistled duets (when nobody else could hear, of course). He told me about the constellations that dotted the black night sky and explained why I could hear conversations that carried over the water from unsuspecting boaters. "Why do you think Jesus told stories from a boat?" he asked. Little "ah ha!" moments peppered my thoughts . . . and all the while I was learning to listen to God.

I know this is not the kind of experience many people have had growing up. Mine was unique and wonderful. The reason I mention it in some detail here is to underscore the fact that my relationship with God has been profoundly influenced by people, like my dad, who were willing to walk along with me. I grew up asking questions and seeking answers, never afraid that such a pursuit would dislodge my faith. After all, doesn't faith mean you dare to trust? How can you call it faith if you never take a risk? And is a faith that can't stand my questions worth having at all?

As I grew up, I met Jesus in the circumstances of my life. Sometimes He was my hero. Sometimes, quite honestly, I limited my thoughts of Him to church. But as I matured and began to deal with the serious issues of life, the faith I had seen in my parents, and had learned to honestly question and then trust as a child, was strong enough to meet my doubts and tears, even my self-inflated intellect, with something that was real. Jesus was real. In time He became my Savior, my Lord, my friend and teacher, just as He had been for my dad.

Knowing Jesus continues to be a journey in which every step has the potential to bring a new lesson about God. This is the walk I am talking about. It's all about what happens after the first time a person realizes Jesus as Lord. What gets people to their next step? What helps them learn to ask good questions and to find valid answers, to think and to trust? What kind of life does God really want us to have, and should our actions and decisions really be influenced by what we say we believe? What does God want from us, anyway?

This last question has bothered God's people for millennia! In the Old Testament God gave rules and laws for the people to obey so they could know Him as a holy God. He established feasts and ceremonies to help them remember the lessons of His faithfulness to them throughout the years, and to help them remember that He is a God who has given a promise of salvation. A God who wants to enter into the everyday experience of His people is unique to the God of the Bible, and people have long tried to find ways to somehow merit or deserve such attention. The problem was, and still is today, that people confuse performance of religious obligations with an actual love relationship with God. Performance-based religion is exhausting and frustrating because the work is never done and our efforts are never enough. When we do this, we tend to zero in with frightening tunnel vision on the requirements of our faith and miss altogether the companionship of a personal God who deeply desires for us to take time to listen and learn of Him.

This struggle with religious requirements is well documented in the history of God's people as it is recorded in the Old Testament. In Micah 6 we read that God's people were so busy trying to do enough to please Him that they were frazzled with despair! Their hearts were not filled with love, only rules and traditions and duty, and God was not pleased. Listen to these words recorded for us by the prophet Micah.

> "With what shall I come before the Lord
>     and bow down before the exalted God?
> Shall I come before him with burnt offerings,
>     with calves a year old?
> Will the Lord be pleased with thousands of rams,
>     with ten thousand rivers of oil?
> Shall I offer my firstborn for my transgression,
>     the fruit of my body for the sin of my soul?" (Micah 6:6–7)

This is the frustration of people who just don't get it! And you can hear this same kind of questioning from good Christian people today.

"I am exhausted! I teach Sunday school and sing in the choir. I homeschool my kids and spend half my time in one carpool or another. We do homework and music lessons and sports, and I always monitor what the kids watch on TV . . . and yet something isn't right. I work hard and I give my time and money to the church. I'm trying to be a success, but I am so tired. I serve on committees and boards, and meetings consume my free time. God, what do you want from me?"

When people feel this unworthy, no matter how much they do, they have forgotten the purpose of the Christian walk. They are doing good and commendable things—things that they know are pleasing to God—but something is out of order.

When God heard the frustration of His people in the days of Micah, He answered with words meant for them, and for us.

> "He has showed you, O man, what is good.
>     And what does the Lord require of you?
> To act justly and to love mercy
>     and to walk humbly with your God." (Micah 6:8)

Hear the word of the Lord: "Walk with Me!"

Walking with God means giving Him control over every aspect of your life. It means listening and questioning, caring enough to develop a relationship that is dear and personal to you. The greatest gift a person can bring into another person's life is the realization of the presence of God, as my dad did with me. Because my dad was intentional about teaching me to think and grow, I grew to know him very well and to trust his input in my life. And as I walked through life with my dad, I realized the presence of God.

It is God's desire that every person learn to walk with Him in close and meaningful relationship. Such intimacy and trust doesn't come easily for people who haven't been shown the care and felt the safe encouragement that some of us have. What about children who have been abused and hurt by the very people who should have been teaching them about God? How can a survivor of neglect or of verbal or sexual abuse at the hand of a father be persuaded to trust God as Father? These are questions that need to be faced and embraced by mature Christians. God hasn't shown favor to some because they have particular merit. No, He has given extra grace to some, fully expecting us to do for young believers and seekers what my dad did for me.

God expects us to live lives of faithfulness and love that are invested in and easily accessible to younger believers. This is discipleship. Christians are given the awesome responsibility of making disciples. Keeping our lives of faith personal and private is not an option. Scripture is written, Genesis to Revelation, around God's promise to bless His people so that the whole world will be blessed through them. (See Genesis 12:2–3.) As children of God we have not been blessed so that we can enjoy keeping the blessing; we have been blessed to pass on that blessing. God's blessings, like manna in the desert, are meant to be used daily and renewed every morning. Hoarded blessings, like day-old manna, lose their sweetness and ability to nourish (Exodus 16:20).

It's all about the walk. We are meant to live in daily interaction with God Almighty—walking, with open eyes, and expecting to see God's presence in exciting and personal ways. And when the "ah ha!" moments of learning and discovering happen, we should have a natural and instant reflex to share them with those who travel along with us.

No one comes to Jesus alone. No one walks with God alone. Those who insist that faith is personal and private are choosing to close their eyes to the many companions God has provided who see Him and learn things from Him that will enrich our lives. Who are the people who have helped you to walk with God? Who is God bringing to your mind that you could turn around and help?

In the following chapters we will identify three key aspects of a healthy walk with God. These are not the three aspects, nor are they a formula for life to the full. Only the presence of Jesus, with us and in us, can bring life to the full. These three necessary roles, however, are noticeable in people who are becoming like Jesus, who are living life to the full . . . extreme life. If you are living in relationship to God through Jesus Christ, you are becoming . . .

## A DISCIPLE

One who embraces and assists in spreading the teachings of another.

## AN INTERCESSOR

One who brings another into the presence of God Almighty by means of prayer, and who brings awareness of the presence of God Almighty into the life for which he prays.

## A MENTOR

One who serves as a wise and trusted counselor or teacher to another person.

# *Chapter Two*

# CALLED TO BECOME
# A DISCIPLE

WHAT DO YOU think when you hear the word *disciple*? Do you come up with words like obligation, rules, suffering, penance, cross-bearing, church attendance? Committee work, guilt, tithing? Building Christian organizations and supporting Christian industries? Doing door-to-door evangelism, giving your testimony, reading Christian books and listening to Christian music? Not going to bars or wild parties, pasting a fish on your bumper? Surrounding yourself and your children with Christian friends? Going to seminars and committing to study the latest book in a small group?

"Is there anything wrong with those things?" you may ask. Nothing! Absolutely nothing. All can have, and many should have, a place in the Christian life and in the church. But they are all things we do, and by themselves they don't get to the heart of what it means to be a disciple. Being a disciple isn't about doing something for Jesus. It's about what Jesus wants to do in us and for us.

When Jesus told us to go and make disciples, He wasn't talking about rounding up a congregation of like-minded people who will behave in certain prescribed ways. Remember, rule-keeping and living by a list of dos and don'ts were exactly the things that upset Jesus about the religious leaders of His day. Not that the rules or lists themselves were wrong, but the fact that they had become the measure of one's faithfulness and had replaced a passionate love for God.

Far too often religious activity draws attention to people and what they can do, not to the person of Jesus Christ. People begin to believe that the religious things they do are somehow things God needs them to do, or are things that give them merit in His eyes. Someone who is walking as a disciple of Jesus Christ has only one legitimate motive for his actions: honoring Jesus. In chapters 5–7 of Matthew, Jesus teaches about specific things that should mark the life of a disciple of Jesus. It is pretty well summed up in Matthew 5:14–17:

> "'You are the light of the world. A city on a hill cannot be hidden. Neither do people light a lamp and put it under a bowl. Instead they put it on its stand, and it gives light to everyone in the house. In the same way, let your light shine before men, that they may see your good deeds and praise your Father in heaven.'"

We are not to shine a light; we are to be the light! Good deeds are not the way we light our lamp or even the way it stays lit . . . good deeds are the natural outcome of a life of discipleship just as light is the natural outcome of lighting a lamp. Jesus was telling the people who crowded around Him that their very identity was to shine forth the essence of God. If you are a disciple of Jesus, when people encounter you their first thought should be to praise your Father in heaven. When they witness a good deed or an act of service that you perform, their response should be, "that reminds me of Jesus!" When that happens, the only explanation is that you are a disciple of Jesus who is becoming more like Him as you walk together.

What about "taking up a cross" to follow Jesus? Well, there just is no way to follow Jesus and avoid the cross. To follow Him means to be willing to go where He went, through the same types of situations He faced, and to take our clues from Him as to how we are to keep walking. It is during the difficult times when our own strength is stretched to the limit that a precious and personal connection with the Savior is formed. But "our cross" is a term that is frequently defined incorrectly. Often we describe a physical ailment, a wayward child, or our circumstances in life as "our cross." And indeed some of our experiences or life circumstances are difficult burdens to bear. But "taking up" one's cross implies a decision to bear the consequences of a choice to follow Jesus. So when we speak or act in accordance with God's Word and by the prompting of the indwelling Spirit and are consequently faced with hardship because of it, then we are truly taking a walk with a cross.

It is unfortunate, however, when we get caught up in the enormity of the burden and the suffering involved. Although Jesus clearly teaches that we need to count the cost of following Him, He never portrays the life of a disciple as joyless, tedious, and filled with religious duty. Those are not characteristics of "life to the full." We need to remind ourselves and each other that following Jesus into difficult situations is only the first half of the trip.

Unless we panic and seek our own escape route, our walk will also follow Jesus out of the difficulty. Nothing about His life ended in defeat. Jesus doesn't lead His disciples into dead ends, and what lies ahead is always better than what lies behind.

Discipleship is dynamic and character-changing. A few Old Testament saints enjoyed extraordinary communication with God. Abram heard God's voice, God spoke with Moses as a man speaks to a friend (Exodus 33:11), Enoch walked with God (Genesis 5:24), the prophets heard from God, and He spoke to other Old Testament heroes. But for the most part, for the ordinary person, access to God was limited in time (special days) and space (special places) and through appointed intercessors (priests and sacrifices). Then, Jesus chose twelve men to be the first to experience a radical new personal relationship with God. They are like our test case for this amazing paradigm shift, where ordinary people were finally welcomed into intimate friendship with God through the atoning work of His Son.

Think of it: Knowing God! Walking with God! Learning from God! Being disciples of God Himself!

When I think of this, I think of an entirely different list of words to associate with the word disciple: excitement, adventure, purpose, danger, challenge, discipline, power, and delight! Really, can you imagine how amazing it must have been following Jesus wherever He went during those three years of His earthly ministry? Sitting around a fire at night, listening to His stories. Walking into towns you had never visited before and having people gather around you just to hear your Friend teach, just to see or touch Him. Watching the word spread through the crowds that because of your Friend's miraculous healing power a blind man could see or a lame man could walk! Looking into the animated, authoritative eyes of the Master Storyteller as His words finally fit the pieces together in your puzzled mind so that you could say, "I get it!" If ever there was an example of life in all its fullness, it has to be the life of the Twelve as they followed and listened to and lived with this incredible Man whom children loved; whom the waves, the wind, and masses of fish obeyed; and who dared to confront the legalism and sin of arrogant and powerful religious authorities.

Then, imagine the day when Jesus called the Twelve together for a little talk and told them they were to go out and do the very things they had seen Him do. Imagine the first time they dared to cast out a demon in Jesus' name . . . and it worked. Imagine them looking at their Rabbi and Friend and having the truth crash in on them: "My God! You actually are my God!"

Discipleship is not easy. It will cost you everything. But "everything" becomes a small price for your investment in the eternal richness of knowing God. Not only does God promise phenomenal return on your investment, but also He provides everything you need to make the investment in the first place, and to pay the cost along the way (2 Peter 1:3).

As evidence we have the well-documented account of these first disciples and the impact their walk with Jesus had on their lives. Other than Judas, these men were transformed, empowered . . . on fire! And after the work of the cross was done and all authority had been given to Jesus, His great instruction to those who followed Him was:

"Keep this up!"
"Make disciples."
"Bring more."
"Walk together and walk with Me."

# Chapter Three

## CALLED TO BECOME AN INTERCESSOR

SOMETIMES I WISH we could have the physical presence of Jesus with us. I think of what a joy it must have been to hang out with this amazing Man, to listen to His stories and watch Him do miraculous things, and I can hardly imagine it! What did the bread taste like that filled up the multitude, or the wine at the wedding in Cana? I think of Mary, Martha, and Lazarus getting things ready because Jesus and a few friends were dropping by for dinner. (What does one cook when Jesus is coming for dinner?) I think of Peter's mother-in-law lying in bed, knowing that Peter was bringing his friends home for dinner but too sick to get up and do anything about it. The door opens, Jesus walks in, and after a little conversation and the touch of His hand, she is feeling just fine. Wouldn't it be amazing to be able to go to Him, newspaper in one hand and the Bible in the other, and ask all the questions that such a contrast brings to mind? How quickly I would run to Him with my children's broken hearts or my friend's incurable illness.

When Jesus was physically here, He could talk to and touch many people, but He confined Himself to physical boundaries. Only so many friends could have His attention. Only so many miles could be covered in a day. Then one day He gathered His friends and told them that He needed to go away so that the Holy Spirit could come to them. When Jesus finished His work, all self-imposed physical boundaries were removed. No longer was He confined to the body and personality of a young Jewish man. Now, through the power of the Holy Spirit who comes to dwell in anyone who believes, He can come and be with anyone, anytime. Jesus doesn't come for dinner in the same way as He did years ago, that's true. But He also doesn't *only* come for dinner . . . having to move on after just a short stay.

Today, prayer is the means by which Jesus visits our hearts and our homes. We're not talking simply about a blessing over a meal or a quiet time in the morning, although those can certainly be wonderful times with God. God hears the simple prayers of the small child who calls out to Him. He heard the voice of the thief on the cross and the Roman centurion whose slave was ill. Simple prayer is where we all start in opening our lives to the influence of God. But a mature prayer life is something much bigger and more enveloping. We're talking about communication that is not begun with "Dear God" like you're writing a formal letter, followed by a list of suggestions or a plan of action. We're talking about the awareness that God has something for you this day that you desire to find.

In a little book titled *The Practice of the Presence of God*, Brother Lawrence, a seventeenth-century lay-servant with the Carmelites, writes about finding God amid the pots and pans in his daily chores. His life and teachings are exceptional simply because they are so ordinary. His simple wisdom and ways were filled with the presence of God, not because he prayed much, but because his life was one unending conversation with God. As He did with Brother Lawrence, Jesus actually lives with us, in our lives and in our homes, and the key to realizing His presence lies in simply remembering that He is there! Such remembering is the beginning of prayer, and prayer is where we begin our walk with God.[1]

Discipleship *cannot* happen and mentoring *should not* happen apart from an active prayer life. So how does one learn about prayer?

Most of us approach God in prayer because we want to be heard. Children keep away scary dreams by reciting "Now I lay me down to sleep. . . ." We thank God for our food and we go to God with our requests. The many habits of prayer and uses of prayer in formal gatherings are sometimes hard to understand, but somehow they convey the idea that respect is being paid to God. That's not a bad thing. Hollywood has given us ample stories of people who call out to God when they are in despair, or make deals with God that they will change if only He fixes the situation they are in. Wherever and however people are compelled to come to God, whether they are little children or wise and educated adults, the invitation to come is open.

I don't remember specifically learning to pray; I only remember praying and listening to prayer as a child. But

---

1. This book is not meant to be a full teaching on prayer. Excellent studies and inspirational teachings are available that can lead you into a deeper understanding of the meaning and the practice of prayer. See Recommended Books on Prayer at the end of the book.

prayer, like any other worthy discipline, needs to mature and increase in scope as it is practiced. When we are beginners, we learn the models and the recitation of specific prayers to help us become familiar with being in the presence of God. As we grow, those models become guidelines and boundaries for our own expressions, and finally we begin to realize the boundless possibilities and the intimate nature of communication with God. The Psalms teach us that there is no emotion that God will not listen to in prayer. He will handle our love and adoration as well as our disillusionment and anger. What He doesn't want from us, however, are "show prayers," such as the ones Jesus pointed out in the temple offered by people who honored themselves with their religious words and actions.

Prayer is necessary for our own personal good and growth, and it is an absolute prerequisite before we attempt to instruct or lead anyone else. Prayer is to the soul what breathing is to the body. When our schedules get full, conscious time in prayer is often the first thing to go.

Have you ever exercised so hard that you momentarily forgot to breathe? That's why exercise instructors yell to their classes, "Breathe, breathe!" Without regular breath, the muscles get fatigued and our performance wears us out. Exhausted, we collapse as our bodies try to recover. Think of the people in your church who go to every program and sit on every committee, running from one Bible study to the next, holding their breath! Not a pretty or a healthy picture. "Breathe, breathe! Pray, pray!"

My own education in prayer has been marked by two significant events, which God used to take me to new understandings of who He is and how I should pray. The first helped me understand that prayer isn't something I do; it's somewhere I go. The second taught me that prayer isn't just what I say, but also what I hear. I share these stories here because these are lessons that have enabled my work in intercessory prayer, teaching me how to bring others to God and how to hear what God would have me say to them.

### A Lesson from Illness: Prayer isn't about getting answers, but about being in the presence of God.

When my youngest son was eight months old, we took a vacation in Florida, enjoying a sunny respite from our New Jersey winter. After a day at the pool, I returned to the room to discover that my face, chest, and arms were a mass of itchy red bumps. Figuring it was an allergic reaction to something, I was careful about what I ate and drank and about my exposure to the sun. A month later, out of the sun and back in the cold Northeast, the rash persisted. Visiting several doctors and undergoing various tests left me with an unwanted diagnosis of Systemic Lupus and a quickly growing condition of fatigue and pain. The doctor warned me to avoid stress and stay out of the sun.

Later that year, during our three-week vacation with the family on the sandy shores of Lake Michigan, I dutifully donned my sunscreen and gigantic ugly hat. On a few of our trips down the long hill to the beach I noticed another young woman wearing a big hat that was nearly as unattractive and uncool as mine. I knew who she was, a neighbor with three little girls, but I didn't really know her. Then one day when I was just too tired to make the trek to the beach, I saw her out in her parents' backyard and went over for a chat. Her name was Karen, and as we struck up a conversation about our hats we quickly found common ground. She was battling breast cancer and had to avoid the sun. Her prognosis was good, but the hat was a pain! My prognosis wasn't clear yet and you already know what

I thought about my hat. We talked about all sorts of pent-up fears . . . about not being sick in front of our kids and not being a burden to our husbands. The conversation was wonderful but short, because she was heading home to Wisconsin that day. But before she left, we made a quick pact: I would pray for her when I felt sick, and she would pray for me when she felt sick.

This was the first time I had ever really given my word to someone that I would pray, and that fall, back in New Jersey, I decided to begin attending a Wednesday night prayer group just for Karen. I still remember the first night of that prayer meeting. After we sang a few old hymns, the pastor, Pastor Jack, launched into a serious work session, standing in front of a whiteboard filled with names. Most of the people in the room were senior citizens who faithfully worked at prayer. They reported on the names that were on the board from previous weeks, sharing accounts of God's comfort and in some cases unexplained healing. They laughed knowingly as they spoke of the "coincidences" in the lives of people as the result of prayer. Then we spent time in joyful prayer, thanking God for the amazing answers on that whiteboard. (I soon learned that people who had nothing to do with the church would call with requests and concerns because word of this powerful prayer group had spread.)

The next order of business was putting new names and circumstances on the board. When Pastor Jack asked if there were any more additions, I felt myself rise to my feet. "I have a friend named Karen who has three little kids, and cancer," I said, and Karen's name was written on the board.

The following half hour or so was a time of earnest prayer, with each item on the board being prayed for with great simplicity and often tears. I was fascinated by an elderly Norwegian woman who kept softly, and with extreme reverence and love, saying, "Jesus, my Jesus." Sometimes there was just silence, and that first night I tried to pray for Karen in the silence, but my mind kept wandering. After all, half an hour was a long, long time!

The next week I was sick, but I tried again to be faithful in praying for Karen. It became evident after only a few days, however, that my attention span was woefully short. About then, someone, and I'm not sure who, gave me a piece of advice: "Picture yourself in the actual presence of God, and bring your friend with you." This helped me to have a focus for my prayers, and the next Wednesday I tried to employ my imagination during the silent prayer time. I pictured the throne of grace . . . at least I tried. I slid off the church bench and knelt on the hard, cold floor. I still remember the feeling of kneeling before God Almighty, feeling small and inconspicuous . . . I wanted so desperately to look up and see Him, but I could only stare at the floor. Somehow in my desire for His presence, God had brought my mind into a place of awe, wonder, and amazement. As I tried to think in words, my mind's eye saw a sandaled foot come and stand before me. Words failed. Again, I wanted to look up and see the face of my Intercessor, but my eyes were glued to the floor. It seemed that in just a few moments that half hour was over, and as we closed the time with a song, the little "Jesus" lady gently touched my shoulder and smiled. As I walked out to my car, I knew that something had changed within me.

Every week I brought Karen with me to that Wednesday night meeting. Every time the place I found to kneel was before the throne of grace, and every time words failed. About all I could come up with was, "God, I'm here with my friend Karen." It was an amazingly satisfying time of prayer! There was nothing I needed to tell God. He already knew.

In the spring I received a letter from Karen saying that the lump her doctor thought would go away had instead grown, and the cancer was spreading throughout her body. Some zealous but ill-informed Christian had told her that she wasn't healed because her faith wasn't strong enough and she wanted to know what I thought. We wrote back and forth, and each time I felt the urgency to run to my place of prayer. It was amazing to me that no matter where I was, I could always just kneel down and be in my own place before the throne . . . with the ever-present sandaled foot and my friend Karen at my side. "God, I'm here and I've brought Karen."

As I headed up to Michigan the next summer I was looking forward to seeing Karen. It was odd. We had spoken to each other only once. We had never prayed together, only promised to pray while we were apart.

When we arrived at the lake, I learned that Karen was leaving that very day to go back to Wisconsin, so I hurried down to her parents' house. Her mom came to the door and greeted me warmly. "Karen has been hoping you would come!" I wasn't ready for what came next. The only part I could recognize about her was her eyes. Her long, thick red hair was gone. Her face was swollen and she sat uncomfortably in a chair. She had been ravaged by a relentless evil, and she lived in constant pain.

We didn't have much to say to each other. "Maybe we should pray," she suggested. I knelt on the floor in front of her chair, took both of her hands in mine, and mumbled some kind of clumsy prayer. It was silent for a while . . . I could hear the clock ticking in the next room. The tears were making big spots on my jeans as I looked at the familiar floor and the comforting sandaled foot. After a time Karen prayed. I can't remember everything she said, but the words she closed with still play like a recording in my memory. "Jesus, we thank you for caring so well for us this year. I know that the next time we are together we will be with you, and we will both be well."

As we looked up and into each other's eyes, Karen smiled and said, "It's funny, but it's so familiar. I know we've done this before." God had bound us together, even though we were nine hundred miles apart, with the same experience of praying at the throne of grace.

Karen left. When I got the letter a few weeks later with the news that she had died, I went back to the Wednesday night meeting to update the whiteboard. As we prayed silently, I found myself once again in my familiar place of prayer. "God, I am here, but this time I'm all alone."

"Perhaps you need to find someone else to come with you now." The words came from a place outside of me, but I heard them as clearly as I heard the voices of those around me. And at that moment, I was profoundly changed.

My first intentional assignment to intercede had taught me that God's answer to any problem is His presence. Prayer isn't a process we go through to end up with the results we desire. Prayer is choosing to spend the time we have very near to the One who created us specifically for the purpose of enjoying His company.

> There is a place of quiet rest, near to the heart of God;
> A place where sin cannot molest, near to the heart of God.
> O Jesus, blest Redeemer, sent from the heart of God,
> Hold us, who wait before Thee, near to the heart of God.
> (Cleland B. McAfee)

Prayer is making the conscious choice to rest, to wait, to find our place close to God's heart. Intercession is our privilege to bring someone along with us to that place.

An intercessor is someone who stands in the gap for someone else. An intercessor faces God—loving, pleading, and caring for someone else—and then invites that person to draw near to God for himself or herself. In this book, that is the scope and the meaning of the word *intercessor*, and it is my contention that to do the job well a disciple must be carefully willing to represent both the need of the one and the sufficiency of the other.

### A Lesson from Silence: Prayer isn't about what you say, but about what you hear.

One of my favorite things about my father was listening to him tell me stories of his life, or sharing in his musings on perplexing thoughts such as the meaning of eternity and time. As I listened to him share his memories and express his thoughts, I found I had more things in common with him than I had ever realized as a child. I truly was my father's daughter, and as he told me about himself, I learned more about myself.

On the day that my dad died, I opened my daily journal of *My Utmost for His Highest*, and the words of Oswald Chambers in that day's reading took my breath away. The Scripture was Isaiah 6:1: "In the year that King Uzziah died, I saw the Lord." My broken and confused heart was stunned by the words that followed:

Our soul's history with God is frequently the history of the "passing of the hero." Over and over again God has to remove our friends in order to bring Himself in their place, and that is where we faint and fail and get discouraged. Take it personally: In the year that the one who stood to me for all that God was, died—I gave up everything? I became ill? I got disheartened? or—I saw the Lord? . . .

It must be God first, God second, and God third, until the life is faced steadily with God and no one else is of any account whatever. "In all the world there is none but thee, my God, there is none but thee."[2]

I tried to pray, but I couldn't . . . or maybe I just didn't want to. What I had to say to God brought me no peace and sounded just like what it was: the ranting of an angry child who felt abandoned and injured. All of the answers I had figured out about life meant little in the aftermath of death. How I missed my father! No one would ever take his place.

But life goes on, as it always does, and I found my way back to routine and work, and even prayer. One day as I sat on the deck, looking across the backyard, memories of long talks with Dad filled my head. The empty chair next to me seemed to invite conversation. It just seemed like a good time to pray. I'm not sure what prompted it, but I looked right at the empty chair and heard myself ask God the same question I had asked my dad hundreds of times. "Father, will you tell me about yourself?" No other words came. No other words were needed. That day I learned to pray expecting an answer.

Suddenly my prayers were directed and informed. What did I know about God? What stories and testimonies had I heard that I actually believed? I went inside and got my Bible . . . I mean, if I wanted to hear what God had to say, wasn't His Word a pretty good place to begin?

I don't have any idea how long that time of prayer lasted, but I remember the experience vividly. I listened. I learned. My heart was comforted. Not by answers to my whining

2. Oswald Chambers, *My Utmost for His Highest*, *Journal*, July 13 (Uhrichsville, Ohio: Barbour Publishing, Inc.).

questions, but rather by the presence of God, right there with me! What I thought was impossible had happened. Once I made it available, God came into and totally filled the place only my dad had filled before. My father's Abba Father had taken His rightful place as my Abba Father as well. A new kind of spiritual intimacy had been ushered into my prayer life. Not only could I come into His presence; I also could listen to Him share His stories, thoughts, and desires.

So why is it important for us as disciples of Jesus to grow in our practice of prayer? And why is it important that we pray for others? Because God invites us into the intimacy of His heart so that we will learn who He is and how to worship Him. When we become confident that He is our loving Abba Father as well as Almighty God, we cannot help but bring others to Him. Andrew, when he first met Jesus, could not help but run and bring his brother. "We have found the Messiah," he said, and he brought Peter to Jesus (John 1:41). We all know how that turned out! This is why every believer needs to be involved in the important work of intercession. It is where we begin when we want to bring somebody to Jesus. It is what we can do to stand beside a struggling new believer or those who cannot pray for themselves. Whether we are bringing them for the first time, for salvation, for healing, or just for love, intercession is where we must begin.

Fully equipped disciples have a mandate to use what God has built into our lives for the purpose of making new disciples and helping them to become like Jesus. On the last night of His life Jesus found the time to pray for you and me (John 17). When that kind of love begins to happen in our hearts, we won't be able to keep from doing the work of intercession.

# Chapter Four

# CALLED TO BECOME A MENTOR

IF EACH PERSON who comes to know Christ would take the words of His Great Commission seriously and make mentoring a personal priority, the church would see a measure of health and power far beyond what we experience today.

> "All authority in heaven and on earth has been given to me. Therefore go and make disciples of all nations, baptizing them in the name of the Father and of the Son and of the Holy Spirit, and teaching them to obey everything I have commanded you. And surely I am with you always, to the very end of the age." (Matthew 28:18–20)

When Christ's redeeming work was done and He met with the remaining eleven disciples, He instructed them on how to represent Him in the world during the time of His physical absence. "Do what you've seen me do," He told them. "As the Father has sent me, I am sending you" (John 20:21).

Evangelism, which is the passionate preaching of the good news of salvation, is our wonderful calling and privilege. Imagine being invited to spend eternity with God and being told we can invite anyone else we want to come too! But our responsibility doesn't end there. Jesus didn't say to go and make converts; He said to go and make disciples . . . and then to baptize them and teach them everything we know about Him. To be baptized is to become identified with a teaching or a person. So we are to walk with those who have decided to follow Jesus until they understand what it means to be identified with Him. Then the adventure begins. Then we can teach them how to obey, how to live, how to walk well with the Teacher.

Too often, however, we have substituted the word *convert* for *disciple* and have allowed ourselves to be satisfied with statistics that tell us how many people are making decisions to follow Jesus. But one doesn't become a disciple by decision alone. One becomes a disciple by truly getting to know the person he or she is following. An ancient saying describes a disciple as one who "is covered in the dust of his rabbi." Disciples were formed as they walked through life with their teacher, becoming like him and identifying with him in every way—covered in his dust. Only by walking daily in step with God is a person changed into a true disciple. It's a lifelong process.

A pastor and friend gave a great illustration of this disciple-making responsibility. "It is such good news when we hear that someone we love who has wanted a child is expecting! We rejoice with them and await the child. We congratulate them and celebrate the new life. Now suppose that once the child is born the new parents take it and set it up on a rock somewhere, happy that it came, but not concerned with its nurture and care. What would we think of the parents then? The same thing applies to the birth of new believers in the church. We cannot be guilty of neglecting their nurture and care." Teaching, sharing, and mentoring help new believers get to know the Savior in an intimate and meaningful way and to hear and understand the lessons God has given us. This equips them to begin living eternally now, in the power of the Holy Spirit. And just imagine what that can do for the life of any church!

Jesus Christ is the original spiritual mentor. During His earthly ministry He called twelve men and poured His life into them. He taught them how common, everyday existence could be transformed through connection and communication with God. He showed them how to walk in faith, how to pray and seek and find. He spoke with them, laughed with them, ate, walked, and traveled with them. He reminded them of who they were in Him and enticed them to think, to ask questions, to know Him intimately and keep learning from Him. He showed them how to do miraculous things and then stood by as they developed their own gifts. Jesus was a friend and a mentor who had time to listen, to love, and to invest His life in His closest followers—both His moments of triumph and His moments of despair.

For an obedient disciple of Jesus Christ, mentoring is not an optional activity. Carrying out the Great Commission means being involved fully in the lives of others the way Jesus was involved in the lives of His disciples. "I am with you always," Jesus assured His followers. That is His example to us. New believers need to be assured of the presence of Jesus in their lives. One of the most powerful ways we experience the presence of Christ is through the company of His disciples.

Jesus' plan was not to build a first-century mega-church that would be caught up to heaven and saved from a fallen world. His plan was for a worldwide church, far beyond anything His disciples could have imagined. And the way His church would be built . . . is still being built . . . is one person reaching out with the gospel to another person, and showing that person how to reach out to the next person, and so on . . . keeping the process going. (Remember the "very real chain of hands connecting you to the nail-scarred hands of Jesus"—chapter 1.)

Walking together is an essential element of Jesus' plan. And at the heart of His plan is His desire for each disciple to make disciples and train them, in turn, how to make disciples. That is what He did. Although He began with the twelve men that He personally touched during His life, our Lord didn't come to save just a small band of men. He came to save the world. And He didn't come to save just their world, but to save the complicated and messed-up world we live in today. The good news has come down to us today because each generation has produced faithful mentors who have followed the example and command of Jesus to keep His plan going. As Leighton Ford said, "Without a successor there is no success."

Listen to Paul's words in Ephesians 2:19–22:

> "Consequently, you are no longer foreigners and aliens, but fellow citizens with God's people and members of God's household, built on the foundation of the apostles and prophets, with Christ Jesus himself as the chief cornerstone. In him the whole building is joined together and rises to become a holy temple in the Lord. And in him you too are being built together to become a dwelling in which God lives by his Spirit."

People who come to Christ are not isolated followers, but fellow citizens. In this we find the key not only to building healthy churches, but to our own personal spiritual health. As we walk with other disciples, as we serve others, we gain something for ourselves: life lessons and spiritual fulfillment in our own private walk with Jesus. There are personal lessons we just cannot learn, no matter how well-read we are or how many degrees we amass, until we are walking through the stuff of life with someone else.

Companionship is a vital part of the Christian walk. We just were not designed to go it alone. Sadly, many have let organized groups and programs take the place of intimate, Christ-centered friendships. This is not to say that programs or groups are wrong, but they are not "the walk." They are stops along the way where we may pick up nourishment or encouragement for the hike. But it is only in the intimacy of friendships with others who follow Jesus that we can show our true selves . . . our scars and our wounds . . . and our victories. Only in such intimacy can we claim God's power to turn everything to the good. And in this kind of walk we see God up close as He sanctifies each experience and each struggle we lay at His feet. As we bear witness to His power in our everyday lives in vulnerable honesty, love, and expectation, we strengthen each other. We offer the arms of Jesus to hold, His tears to comfort, His encouragement to keep on. And when we do, we see miracles and incredible "coincidences" . . . the stuff of life that makes us gasp in wide-eyed wonder.

"This is awesome!" should be a prayer we breathe not once in a lifetime, but regularly. Over and over, our walk together should reveal more and more of the awesomeness of the God we worship and serve.

Playing half-heartedly at a dull religion is an insult to God. That was never His intent for us. What He has always desired for us is life to the full—ultimate, complete, God-filled life.

I wish I could look right through this page, directly into your face, and let you see the fire that burns in my heart. I wish you could hear from my voice, not my fingertips, that God will enter your day in life-changing ways, and that once you get a taste of a Savior-soaked existence you will never settle for anything less. There is life in Christ that permeates your thinking as the Holy Spirit reminds you of truth after truth that has lain hidden inside you, just waiting for you to access the files. Each truth you have learned, each bit of the Word you have read, and each experience of your life becomes vital, valuable, and living information that informs your walk and opens your eyes to the fact that you don't have because you have stopped asking (James 4:2).

I have found that God's most effective way of connecting His Word with my life is through conversation . . . with Him (Bible study and prayer) and with other believers (discipleship/spiritual mentoring). Spiritual mentoring is not just something I do for someone else. It is God's most direct avenue for educating and blessing me.

No kidding! I can honestly say that I have never been left unchanged after an experience of spiritual mentoring. Every time you make the investment, every time you allow God to use your heart, every time you connect with someone, identifying yourself as a fellow disciple, you will learn something new about the character of God, and you will recognize more of His character in yourself. The lessons He gives you to pass on will increase your own appetite for a more Spirit-filled life. Through obedience to this call you will learn to loosen the grip you have on your things, your time, and your life, and you will find your hands properly open to receive more of God's riches than you can keep to yourself.

Don't be afraid of reaching out to a younger believer or attaching yourself to an older believer in a mentoring relationship, for in doing so you are entering into an association "so that [you] may be one as [Jesus and the Father] are one, " as Jesus prayed for you (see John 17). Remember, God hasn't asked anything of you that He will not amply equip you to do . . . and to enjoy!

## Preparing for and Initiating Mentoring Relationships

I have met many wonderful believers who feel a desire to mentor someone younger in the faith, but are frustrated because they don't know where or how to begin. Remember: Every Christian has some particular, valuable gift he or she can give to God by investing in the life of another. You have something to offer that may change the course of someone's life . . . perhaps even their eternal life. So here are a few guidelines that may help you prepare your heart and begin your adventure.

### 1. Feed Yourself First

What can you offer? How do you find abundant, passionate life in the day-to-day grind of ordinary living? How do you obey Jesus and make disciples? The very first step is the foundation for all the rest, and without it you will not be prepared to make disciples. Without this first step, the most you can hope to offer someone else is your own personal best . . . not God's best.

The first step is to take care of your own spiritual health and vitality.

Sitting on the runway, waiting for a plane to take off, every passenger hears the "airplane safety and survival" speech. Sometimes it's on video for us to watch. You know the scene . . . the calm, clean, well-dressed passengers are sitting bolt upright in their chairs when the oxygen masks drop. As they calmly reach for the mask, we, the likewise calm passengers, are instructed in how to cover our mouth and nose, begin the flow of oxygen with a quick jerk of the tube, and then breathe normally. Then there is always the following imperative: "If you are traveling with a small child or someone who will need your help, put your own mask on first, then assist them."

"What an obvious, useless instruction, I know that!" you might think. No, it's probably the best piece of advice in the whole speech. Someone traveling with a child is naturally prone to reach for the child's mask first. Your first thought is to secure your child's mask . . . you'd use duct tape if you had it . . . and make sure he or she is safe. But what happens to such a selfless parent? As you begin your heroic efforts in an oxygen-depleted atmosphere, the lights go out and Junior is left to fend for himself with an unconscious, albeit well-meaning adult slumped beside him.

Before you set out to mentor others, you need to remember a similarly obvious yet crucial instruction: the first and greatest commandment is to "Love the Lord your God with all your heart, soul, mind and strength." Only when you do that will you be able to effectively love your neighbor as yourself (see Matthew 22:37–40). Your greatest privilege as a child of God is to share your thoughts and your heart, moment by moment, with your heavenly Father and to absolutely immerse yourself in His presence and His Word. It takes time with God before going to Him is your natural first reaction in a time of crisis.

A child of the Almighty Creator God has no business settling for boring faith or an ordinary walk. If the only testimony you have to God's faithfulness in your life is about your first step of faith years ago, if you don't have something new from last week or even last month, you need to revive your own spiritual life. This is not selfishness; it's absolutely necessary if you want to bear the name of Christ. A sure sign that a person is a true disciple of Jesus is her insatiable appetite for the Word of God and her desire to soak her mind in God's thoughts. I can never imagine myself saying that I have had enough of God or that I have learned enough from His Word or that I am satisfied with my spiritual experience.

Please don't misunderstand me. I am totally satisfied with God . . . no doubt about that. He is everything my soul has ever longed for. But until I am joined with Him, there will always be one more step I can take to know Him better. There will always be things I have yet to see and hear and trust. Until the Spirit that lives within me has shown me everything there is to know about Jesus, and I have become exactly like Him, I will always have another step to take.

So the first step to abundant living in Jesus is the hunger for more. Someone who has tasted and seen that the Lord is good (Psalm 34:8) will find that she has an absolutely insatiable craving for more and more of Him, until life is only Him.

Once this happens, you will be compelled to invest your life in the lives of those coming up after you. As you discover new truths, new mercies, new evidence of the living God, you become equipped (and excited) to give relevant and current witness to the fact that God is! A person who is experiencing God Almighty on weekday mornings and Saturday afternoons will find that sharing her life becomes the encouragement young believers are craving! This is real.

Let me repeat this crucial piece of information: Feed yourself first, or the best you can hope to offer to anyone else is just your own personal best . . . and as good as you might think that is, it will not nourish or satisfy a heart that is hungry for God. To be a disciple of Christ, you must be constantly connected to your Source. Jesus made sure His disciples understood this principle when He gave them the picture of Himself as the vine and them as the branches. Just as a branch that is not connected to the vine cannot bear fruit, cannot even live, so the disciple must live in constant connection with Jesus. He continued:

> "'As the Father has loved me, so have I loved you. Now remain in my love. If you obey my commands, you will remain in my love, just as I have obeyed my Father's commands and remain in his love. I have told you this so that my joy may be in you and that your joy may be complete. My command is this: Love each other as I have loved you.'" (John 15: 9–12)

Remaining in Christ means constantly nurturing your faith, and the outcome of such a discipline is joy. Complete joy. We talked earlier about life to the full being discovering what God had in mind when He made you, and becoming that. There just is no bigger joy.

### 2. Make Time for God

We live in a fast-paced world of overcommitted schedules—more commitments than will fit on our calendars, more opportunities than a reasonable person can handle . . . and all such good things! Solve this with your daily planner. When I first began seriously setting aside time for personal nourishment and prayer, which are prerequisite to mentoring, I discovered a trick I will pass on to you. (Satan will use every trick in the book to make you fail. Why not use whatever appropriate tricks you can find to help you be faithful?)

Suppose I have decided to meet a business associate or a friend for coffee at 10:00 at the local coffee shop. I remember the appointment because I have written it down, and I wouldn't think of not showing up. I would never leave a friend waiting. So I began my effort at faithfulness by writing Jesus in on my calendar. (I'm serious here!) Thursday, 10:00–12:00, coffee with Jesus. It might sound silly to you, but I'm telling you it worked for me! When I started treating the nourishment of my soul with the same respect I had for the nourishment of my social life or my body, I found this was an appointment I couldn't forget.

Once you get in the habit of making time with God a regular event, He will show you ample reasons to maintain your discipline. Even if you begin with just a few minutes, if you can give your total attention to God in those minutes and ask Him to increase your faithfulness, He will.

### 3. Make Prayer a Habit

I don't understand how prayer works, but I have seen undeniable evidence of its power. Don't be put off by the fact that you are doing something that is beyond your understanding. I think nothing of flipping on the lights at night because I need relief from darkness. It makes little difference that I can't explain electricity to you or that I really can't grasp the concept of how power is transmitted from some distant transformer to this exact switch. All I know is that when I go to the source, the light comes on. So it is with prayer. God says pray, so we pray. The power becomes evident as we learn to rely on the Source. God will hear your love and your concern and will act on behalf of those you bring before Him.

### 4. Dare to Expand Your Prayer Life

As you become accustomed to bringing others and their needs to God, make sure you also spend time listening. Too often we come to God with demands and suggestions, reports of the way things are in our lives, and advice on how He might deal with situations. All that is needed from you to intercede for another is that you speak the name of this beloved child of God in His presence and that you wait and listen.

It takes patience and time to learn to listen in prayer, but as you do, God will supply everything you need to speak into the life of the person He has pressed upon your heart and mind. Words of encouragement, hope, guidance, help, and comfort that agree with His own written Word will infuse your prayers with purpose and inform any conversations you may have with this person. Being an intercessor doesn't mean you give your own best advice to the situation. So until you hear from God, just keep praying.

### 5. Dare to Start Something

Most of the problems we have with our walk are not with our intentions but with our beginnings. We have an enemy who loves nothing more than to distract us and make us feel like failures. First he will bombard you with reminders of your own shortcomings, trying to make you doubt with thoughts like, "What do I have to offer?" Answer these doubts with truth. God has asked us to make disciples, and He doesn't demand the impossible. Can you listen? Can you pray? Can you point to Jesus? Then you are qualified. Put the doubt behind you and move on. The funny thing is, some of the most valuable lessons we have to pass on to younger believers are the stories of God's faithfulness in our mistakes and failures. Peter is one of my favorite Bible heroes simply because I can relate to his failures and God's restoration.

"But who would want me as a mentor? Who has time to waste hanging out with me? I'm afraid to even approach anybody about this!" Let me give you a bit of truth to use against this lie, learned from years of mentoring experience with young adults . . . and some not-so-young adults. People like to be noticed. Start there. In your prayer time, ask God to give you an idea of where to start, and then watch and listen.

### 6. Use Every Trick in the Book to Help You Be Faithful in Prayer

Most of us who have the desire to mentor another person don't have a problem with wanting to be faithful. We don't fail because we're not faithful; we fail because we are so forgetful!

Write the name (or names) God gives you as you notice people and begin to bring them to your time of prayer. Use your day planner again and designate a certain day as the day you will be faithful to pray for a particular person (I will pray for Joe on Tuesday). Now you have something to offer. "Hey, Joe, can I talk to you for just a minute? God keeps bringing your name to my mind, so I've been praying for you every Tuesday. I just wanted you to know that on Tuesdays somebody is praying for you." You'll be amazed at the response you get. Intercession opens doors to people's hearts.

If you don't use a day planner, write the name of the person and the time you will pray on a note and stick it to the dashboard of your car or on your bathroom mirror, or type the name into the screensaver of your computer. Or how about asking a friend to hold you accountable? The important thing is to have a daily reminder. Get creative! If you set your mind to remembering, you'll find a way.

### 7. Watch for Opportunities and Take Them

As you pray for Joe on Tuesday, listen. God may give you a word from His Word . . . an experience in your life . . . a joke . . . who knows what? Listen and be faithful to pass on what you hear that you know is from God. This will require you to find a way to make contact with the person you are praying for—unobtrusively but faithfully.

With the younger generations, if you can get permission to e-mail them only once a week, and if you keep those e-mails short, your mentoring relationship is begun. Or, you may find some other way to let them know on their day that their name has been spoken in the presence of God. A phone call, or even a wave on Sunday mornings, or a cup of coffee together at a coffee shop once a month might be welcome.

Dear friends, if you can get this far . . . promising to pray and to report what you hear in prayer . . . you have been a total success and totally obedient. God will move your relationship along as you respect those you pray for and offer yourself, your time, your availability, even your vulnerability. As you do this over time, you will find you have earned the right to speak into these individual lives. And you will be amazed how, over time, their lives begin to speak into yours!

Over time . . . here is where we are most likely to fail. Faithfulness is something that happens over time. So be patient and stay faithful. If you can do that, through the witness of the Holy Spirit those you pray for will begin to recognize answers to prayer, will see your uncommon love and acceptance, or even the presence of the fruit of the Spirit in your life. You can also offer them the possibility of a safe relationship.

Some people are obviously ready to connect, but this is not always the case. Learn to read the situation the way it actually is, not the way you want it to be. Pray first. Then pray more. If you put on your holiness persona and approach someone you don't know well with words like "Bible study, discipleship, and mentoring," you'll build a wall between you that might never come down. So set your holy talk aside if you want to connect with people. What they will open up to is your love.

Young people, for example, are craving attention and want desperately to be taken seriously. Find simple ways of building a relationship with them. Remember their names. Ask about their lives. Then (and this is important) remember what they say, and the next time you see them or have contact with them, comment or follow up on it.

Keep your conversations (at least initially) short. No one likes to be dominated or overwhelmed. Sometimes your mentoring opportunity will come about simply because you smiled or waved, said hi, or went to watch an event in which the person is involved. Being a mentor isn't necessarily being a best friend . . . certainly not right away. Leave before they wish you would. Remember, this is not about you; it is about demonstrating the faithfulness of God in your life and offering to walk alongside someone.

You're going to love this!

# Chapter Five

# AN ADVENTURE IN SPIRITUAL MENTORING

MY PARTICULAR CALLING is to pray and to encourage people in Jesus' name. In doing so, I intercede for many. Some of those prayer relationships have, through the years, become adventures in spiritual mentoring, although not everyone for whom I pray has or even wants that type of relationship with me. Whether they do or not, that's God's business. What He has asked of me is that I make a serious investment in prayer and that I make my life, more specifically my heart, available for His use.

Over time (remember that phrase?), God has multiplied my list of people to the point where I need to have some order so that I don't forget anyone and so that each person is reminded of God's love one day a week. As of this writing, my "kids" (that's what I call them) number in the hundreds. Some I mentor; some mentor me. Some are spiritual giants, some are babes, and some are still wondering about the God who cares enough to bother me with their names over all these years. Remember: This is about walking together.

The rest of this book consists of some of the letters I've written to my kids over the years (more about this in the next chapter). They reflect days of delight, days of insight, days of darkness and struggle, and days of noticing the majesty of God. If you are getting started with a mentoring relationship, I suggest you use the stories and thoughts God has given me as a connection point until you begin hearing Him give you your own.

What you will find here is akin to overhearing a conversation or stumbling into someone else's private moment only to find that you are the intended audience. All I have to give you is my testimony of what God has taught me about being a mentor. This offers you a peek into the heart of an ordinary disciple who has been asked by God to have regular discussions with Him about other ordinary people, with extraordinary results.

How does God write His words on an ordinary heart? You'll be amazed! As you learn to come and ask, and then wait with open eyes and ears, His language will become as natural to you as the language you use in your own thoughts. He longs to encourage those He loves, and He wants to pass the message of encouragement on through you and me. It isn't a difficult thing, and as you commit your energies to the love and service of those God leads to you, you may be astonished that the one who receives the lion's share of blessing is you. You will learn to listen and hear. Although this book is about the imperative to make disciples (of Jesus) and to walk with them, it is first and foremost about becoming a better disciple yourself.

As I write, I pray for each one whose eyes take in these words. Life to the full is fully possible! Don't settle for anything less.

The wonderful word Paul uses in Romans 12:1, *parakaleo*, translated as "beseech" or "urge" in most translations, means to ask, beg, plead, comfort, exhort, urge, call, invite, encourage. That's what a fellow disciple does. That is what Jesus commanded us to do for each other. Don't be so consumed with your own walk, so busy watching your own feet and checking your own path that you forget the one who may be stumbling along behind you.

Only the humble in heart are satisfied to come alongside. Pride will cause us to seek titles and honors, positions of authority and prestige. But disciples are never elevated above the teacher (John 13:16–17). Jesus has called us "to do as I have done for you" . . . to make disciples . . . and to be disciples . . . and to serve disciples. What higher calling is there than to wash feet, to come alongside, to encourage someone in following Jesus?

Mother Teresa said that we are not called to be successful, only faithful. God delights in faithful hearts. And God is faithful.

Come on!

## Chapter Six

# JUST FOR YOUR INFORMATION

THE FINAL PAGES of this book hold a collection of letters, written in response to times of prayer for my kids. I hope you will find encouragement there. I hope you will write letters yourself or share mine. The whole point is to have conversation with each other about God. These are just letters from me, written on good days, bad days, gray days, and silly days. God is in every one if we just take the time to notice. Just for your information, this is how the letters came to be . . . .

### How It All Began

I didn't know I wanted to pray. I didn't know I was any good at it. Sometimes God needs to take us completely by surprise in order to show us the true desires of our hearts. This is how I learned that I was born to pray.

Several years ago I had a dear friend who seemed to understand my heart, and I his. He had a passion for finding ways to introduce the reality of a walk with Jesus into the lives of young people, even if they didn't know they wanted to know Him. This friend was gifted in a very specific field and figured that if God had supplied ample love and passion for ministry, he intended him to use whatever natural talents and abilities he found at his disposal. My friend played basketball, and had an amazing ability to inspire and teach kids. So he began a business that focused on "teaching excellence in basketball and life" and I was happy to come on board for the specific purpose of loving and praying for the people God brought to us.

One summer God brought us thirteen teenagers from Ireland, and we arranged for each player to stay with a Christian family for the nineteen days of their visit. These kids hadn't come to America to hear about God or to do Bible study. Many of their parents wouldn't have sent their children to anything that was "American evangelical Christianity." We decided that we would let them experience the love of God through our actions and by welcoming them into our homes, but that we would be sensitive to the purpose of their trip and the trust of their parents and only share our personal experience of walking with God as God prompted. Before the kids came, the host families met to study exactly how one can be a witness without words. And we prayed a lot!

When the kids arrived, we were having a really hot summer in North Carolina. We drove them to local gyms at all hours of the day and night. We washed smelly workout clothes and packed really big lunches. We went to the mall, watched baseball, ate family style in local restaurants, and took our kids to water parks and wherever else we had already planned to go with our own families. I mention all this because it was during that time with the Irish kids that God kindled an unexpected love in my heart for them and that my journey of mentoring and discipleship began.

Teillo, the young man who lived in our home, was especially interesting to me. Half Japanese and half Irish, he had exceptional poise and a sense of inner strength. He accompanied our family on several outings, and I found the time I spent with him to be totally enjoyable. I prayed for all the kids, but Teillo found a special place in my heart. As the time of his departure was drawing near, I wondered if God would have me speak of His love in a more specific way. I prayed, "Lord, please use me to show these kids how much you love them"—and an odd thing happened. Tears began to flow. I wasn't sad, but the tears kept softly coming (and I was not a person given to much crying back then). They came as I drove to practices and as I sat and watched the kids play. They came as I listened to stories and as I laughed at jokes. My heart had been profoundly touched, and I was experiencing a love unlike anything I had found for people outside of my own family.

Two days before the group was to head back to Dublin, I asked Teillo if we could go for a walk in a nearby park. As we drove to the park, he asked me about the ring I wore on a chain around my neck. "It belonged to my dad," I told him. This exchange gave me a wonderful opportunity to explain what was so amazing about my dad (a story peppered with faith and trust). I told him that my dad had died a few years back, and then I added, "I hope you can meet him someday."

The rest of the conversation was easy. Teillo talked about his life, his family, and his dreams. He asked questions about mine. I asked if he would be offended if I sent a Bible home with him because he had come to mean a lot to me and I wanted to give him something that was important

65

to me. God didn't direct the conversation to a deeper level, but I did explain briefly what I meant about him meeting my dad one day, hoping Teillo could see my confidence that this was something I fully expected to happen. That day, a friendship began that continues to this day.

As we stood at the airport saying goodbye to these amazing kids, one of them asked me about my tears. "It's the strangest thing!" I said. "A couple of days ago while I was praying for you, I asked God to use me to show you how much He loves you. I've been crying like this ever since. These aren't sad tears, but they just keep coming. What do you make of that?"

The only girl in the group was a beautiful redhead named Gillian. I liked her very much because she could hold her own with a dozen male players. There hadn't been much opportunity for me to spend time with her, however, and as we hugged goodbye I told her that I really wanted the chance to get to know her. She told me that she would remember that, and I had no idea what a special part of my life she would become.

I promised the kids that I would pray for each of them every day until I saw them again, and that is how God began my education in matters of the heart and intercession. This experience of tears is something I tenderly refer to as "the day God broke my heart because it just wasn't big enough." The love that was overtaking me wasn't mine. It was God's love for His children, and since my heart had become a willing vessel, He did what needed to be done. Actually He has kept this process going for years now, breaking and remaking this heart, each time expanding my memory, my time, and my love to include more of His children. Prayer became a joy, and remembering to pray became as natural as remembering to breathe. God's Spirit enables a willing heart to overcome weaknesses that human effort finds insurmountable.

Meanwhile, I became a regular member of the staff at the gym as my friend coached. I fetched towels, ice bags, and Gatorade and cold water for thirsty players. I drove truckloads of basketballs and players from one gym to another. I attended practices and games in the local high schools, getting to know the parents, coaches, and kids. As I sat on the bleachers on a Saturday morning with a group of parents, I'd ask, "Which one is yours?" Eager for someone who would listen, parents would light up as they pointed out and then bragged a bit about their child.

And when they asked me, "Which one is yours?" I would say with a smile, "Well, I guess they're all mine." Then I'd explain that I was on staff and my job was to love and pray for the kids. For the most part these parents were eager to have someone pray for them and their children.

A natural outcome of intercessory prayer is a deep and abiding love, and as my heart kept accepting new kids to love, prayer became my real job—a natural way to spend my mornings. My friend the coach, who had the respect of the players on his court, kept the focus on the pursuit of excellence, but pointed the players to God, to truth, and occasionally to me for prayer and a listening ear. "I'm here to ride you and make you better. I will push you and yell at you. Jan is here to handle the hurts with gentleness and to pray. Get to know this lady." Such strong but subtle assurance spoke volumes to anyone who listened . . . including me.

It is hard to explain exactly how God teaches us about prayer. But prayer is more than a nice thought or a litany of words. Prayer exposes the heart both to the brokenness of human hearts and to the perfection of Almighty God. I believe that God prepares individual hearts step by step in matters of prayer and that we learn how to pray as we pray.

The Holy Spirit speaking to God the Father in the name of Jesus through the instrument of a human heart is a holy thing to experience. The natural arrogance that many of us have experienced in times of prayer . . . that which bids us ramble on in endless recitation of facts or religious jargon . . . is slowly displaced as God gently reveals to us over time who He is and who we are. Talking is replaced by listening, and as we learn that we are simply an instrument of prayer, we begin to discern the very voice of God.

Intercession must precede any other action taken on God's behalf. If we haven't taken the time to learn to recognize the voice of God in the stillness, the best we can hope to offer anyone else is our own best effort. Although we can begin mentoring relationships by giving our own best effort, a relationship that is truly inspired by God will demand our own ongoing education in prayer. With His love, God fuels and informs our practice of prayer, and with His love He compels us to do more than pray. S. D. Gordon wrote, "You can always do more than pray, but never until you have prayed."

As the years passed, God added name after name to my prayer list: basketball players, teenage girls from my Bible study at church, exchange students, college students, ministry leaders, people I met at seminary and at conferences and camps where I spoke and taught. The number of young adults who filled my heart became almost unreasonable, yet I was amazed to find I could remember them . . . and I actually loved them.

Easy Internet access became a wonderful tool for keeping in touch personally with all of my "kids," who now represent eleven countries and the whole span of the U.S. As ministry took me to new places, God would let me know with the sign of those wonderful tears that it was time to squeeze one more of His beloved children into my heart.

Sometimes the breaking and remaking was difficult. The need for a system of remembering became evident.

One day as I sat in a seminary class on worship, my professor told of a man whose ministry was intercession, and he had found a way to organize his prayer life. I was fascinated! He had written out a prayer meant to direct the heart of an intercessor in the manner taught by Jesus. The prayer was written out so that on days when he didn't feel like praying, he had help in being faithful. This was exactly the tool I needed. I began using this prayer plan immediately and have found it very helpful. Here's how it works:

1. My very first order of business before the Lord is my own heart and attitude, and so I begin with this prayer:

   "God, as I open my conscious and unconscious life to your Holy Spirit, pervade my entire being so that I might be wholly sanctified and continually purged and cleansed, so that I might be rightly related to you."

2. Next I add these intercessory words:

   "Father, hear the names of these, your beloved, whom I bring to you."

3. Now I move to the individual names of those I am praying for on that particular day. I have a page that is divided into the five days of the week, and under each day is space to write the names of the people assigned to that day.

4. I use this prayer to guide my thoughts about each person and about myself:

   "May your name be hallowed and revered in my life and the lives of these I have called before you.

   May your sovereign will reign over them and me.

Bend my and their wills to conform to your will.

May each of us receive your daily gifts of providence and enjoy them, and give thanks for them.

Forgive us and help us to forgive others as completely as you have forgiven us.

Keep us from evil, from all beguilement, from the snare of the Evil One.

May we realize your present and coming kingdom.

May we know your power and glory, this day, and forever. Amen."

As I began to follow this plan, I made my lists. Monday would be my girls. Tuesday would be my boys. I wrote to my Monday girls and told them the plan. With their permission I would put them on my Monday list. These were the rules:

I promised to pray for them every Monday.

If God pressed a thought or a Scripture into my heart as I prayed, I would e-mail it to them.

They needed to remember every Monday that their name was being spoken in conversation with God, and that they were loved.

They never needed to respond, but were always welcome to do so.

I would never forward "cute" things, only personal messages, and anyone could ask me to remove them from the list at any time.

For me, the pure gold of this system was that it brought built-in accountability to my spiritual discipline. You see, I had found that I will honor my promise to someone else better than I honor my own good intentions. It's not that I am not faithful; it's just that I am forgetful. With my prayer promises laid out in habitual order, however, it was possible to remember and to keep my word.

What began with two Irish kids, Teillo and Gillian, has continued for nine years as of this writing. I have remembered to pray and have kept in touch with "my kids" every week, and when I hear from them my heart wells up with the same love, the same tears as the first time God answered my prayers for them. And the kids and the stories have multiplied!

God has shown me that the best witness I can offer is faithfulness in love and prayer. The best gift I have to give is my time, and to allow God's love to reach out to others through me.

Because of this intercession, I have become a mentor to some of my "kids," and some of them have mentored me![3] In an age when, for one reason or another, many people find themselves outside of the organized church, it is imperative that faithful disciples of Jesus make their hearts available to love, pray, and speak of the love of God outside the church. Some are called specifically to minister there . . . to point to Jesus and to walk with God's beloved children as an extension of His church until they can find their way back.

It is my prayer that as you read this, and the letters that follow you are thinking, "I can do that!"

Yes, you can.

---

3. God's additional blessing to me . . . something I now know saved my life . . . came about during some years of illness and great personal struggle. I came to a dark place in my life where I could no longer pray for myself, but because I had made a promise to my kids, I brought them into God's presence regularly. Every time I brought them, I brought myself. And because some of those relationships had become dear and trusted, God used them to give me words of love and hope. I will be forever grateful to those who loved me during those dark and difficult days.

# *Letters*

## TO "MY KIDS"

## New Year

What are your plans for the new year ahead of you? I have several specific goals, but I'll share just one with you: I want to learn not only to act like Jesus, but to *react* like Jesus.

This is a huge goal for me. When I have an opportunity to pray or teach, I can usually remember to act somewhat like Jesus. The challenge comes when things are out of my control and hit me from behind. Ah, then, if only I could react like Jesus. If only my instincts and gut reactions were kind, confident, and loving! If only forgiveness came naturally and from my heart. The only way I can see this happening is for me to stay out of the way and let God's Spirit totally take control.

What would happen if we really brought our lives to God in prayer . . . I mean as a serious part of our decision-making?

It is my prayer that you and I enter the New Year confident of the fact that God adores us and has arranged for us to live with Him.

Walk this day in the confidence that God purposely created you as you are (you are no mistake) and that He has promised to supply everything you need to become like Him.

> "His divine power has given us everything we need for life and godliness through our knowledge of him who called us by his own glory and goodness. Through these he has given us his very great and precious promises, so that through them you may participate in the divine nature and escape the corruption in the world caused by evil desires." (2 Peter 1:3–4)

## Perpetual Childhood?

The sun is out this morning and I'm realizing just how much I have missed it on these gray winter days.

Last night some friends and I were discussing Luke 2:41–52, the story about Jesus when He was twelve years old and got left behind in the big city by His parents. (The original *Home Alone*?) It's one of those stories that is easy to skip through and think, *Oh, I already know this.* But we read through the story slowly, looking for Luke's purpose for even recording this in the Scriptures.

We can't do a deep study here, but I urge you to read the story (it's only eleven verses) and try to see things through eyes that want to learn. Here are some of the things we discovered:

1. God loved us enough to set aside His total strength and power and knowledge . . . and to learn it all over again from our perspective. Jesus was a kid here . . . deep into puberty . . . and learning about Himself.

2. It's okay to be struggling and learning . . . Jesus went through that. It's okay to be in process!

3. Maybe being Christlike makes more sense for us if we start by trying to imitate a twelve-year-old Jesus rather than a thirty-three-year-old Messiah. So often we come to faith and expect ourselves to BE THERE and know it all. That's not the way to begin.

4. Jesus looked to His elders for help. Age brings experience, and there is much we can learn from the older people in our lives. (Which gets harder and harder for me as I am becoming one of the old ones!) Church and traditions are where we learn the ancientness of our faith. Christianity

is not a postmodern invention. It is not something "new and improved" but rather ancient and perfect—and worth our thought and study. No matter how old we get, we'll never get to a place where we know enough to stop coming to God as a child.

So, today I hope you see yourself as a child, and I hope you are okay with that. God certainly is. Jesus (the grown man) told people that if we don't come to Him as a child, we will not even enter His kingdom.

Enjoy this day.

"And Jesus grew in wisdom and stature, and in favor with God and men." (Luke 2:52)

## Is Gray a Color?

It's a bit gray outside my window, and I'll admit that it's a bit gray inside as well. I'd blame it on being Monday, or on too much work to do, or on having stayed up too late, but none of those are the real reasons.

I just read this: "The mystery of God is not in what is going to be; it is now." Hmm . . . now.

I don't feel like having devotions. I don't feel like praying. How do I get right on a day like this? Here's the plan. I'll go to God and take you all with me. I'll read a little from the Psalms . . . maybe turn up some music or walk my dogs . . . and look for the mystery of God in my life now. This is discipline. This is practicing when you don't want to . . . working out when you would rather veg out. And days like this, strangely enough, are when we get strong.

I'm writing this to you because I know you face gray days, too. Sometimes we need to be encouraged and inspired by great thoughts of God. But sometimes—like today—we just need to get through the gray.

God is not shocked that you occasionally have a gray day. And never think He is somehow removed from you when you don't "feel" Him there. The mystery of God is not in what is going to be "on a better day." It is now.

I need to go work out. I'll bet this is what Paul was talking about when he wrote:

> "Therefore, my dear friends, as you have always obeyed—not only in my presence, but now much more in my absence—continue to work out your salvation with fear and trembling, for it is God who works in you to will and to act according to his good purpose." (Philippians 2:12–13)

## Fresh Start

I've got great news! Exciting, actually. Here it is: Today is a fresh new day. God has promised to wipe out every mistake and every sin and to give us a fresh new day. God's compassion is "new every morning; great is your faithfulness," writes Jeremiah, the Old Testament prophet.

No matter what happened yesterday or last week, remember that today really is fresh and God doesn't keep score.

Don't you wish we had control of what we remember from yesterday? It amazes me that we choose to carry guilt and failure and blame into fresh days. If this is one of your annoying tendencies, I encourage you to let it go. Someone once said that God invites us to throw our sin into the sea of His forgetfulness . . . and then He puts up a "NO FISHING" sign. Hey, if you've asked God to forgive something, do you really think He'd carry it over to another day?

My friends, today is a clean slate. You haven't messed it up. The only thing you begin with is a God who loves you and wants this to be your best day so far. I'm not talking positive thinking here. I'm just giving you a fact. What you do with it will determine how this day goes.

> "Because of the Lord's great love we are not consumed, for his compassions never fail. They are new every morning; great is your faithfulness." (Lamentations 3:22–23)

## Flying Squirrels

God has such creative ways of reminding me of what's important.

Last night I was out on the deck watching a whole bunch of little flying squirrels fight over our bird feeder. They are so small that they can sit on our "squirrel-proof" feeder and not trip the weight bar that closes the access to the food. One would be eating and another would climb up the tree, fly to another tree, scamper back across the lawn, and launch a sneak attack.

Flying squirrels! I wonder . . . did God create them just to make Him smile?

Then I thought about something else God created for His pleasure. Me. And you. (Check out Colossians 1:16; Revelation 4:11.) He also created us to enjoy Him forever. We do this by praising Him and worshiping Him and communicating with Him in prayer—for ourselves and for each other.

If only we could remember to live our lives for the audience of One! All the other stuff is just other stuff.

May you know what God had in mind when He made you—and do it for all you're worth . . . for the audience of One.

Just this once, don't do something to please someone else, or to further your career, or to make yourself look good. Today find something you can do just for Him, and totally enjoy doing it.

> "He [Jesus] is the image of the invisible God, the firstborn over all creation. For by him all things were created: things in heaven and on earth, visible and invisible, whether thrones or powers or rulers or authorities; all things were created by him and for him." (Colossians 1:15–16)

## Struggling

I'm struggling with a thought today. The first commandment says that we should have no other gods before God, right? Is it actually possible to love God best, most, first, and only? What is at risk when we ask Him to remove anything that we might love or honor more than we honor Him?

When the commandments were given to Israel, the people around them were worshiping other gods. Pagan deities were thought to be the heads of pantheons, or groups of gods, who had power over specific things, such as the rain or fertility. People sacrificed their riches, sometimes even their children to win the favor of these gods. On the pagan holy days the statue of the deity was brought out before the people and the other lesser gods were placed before him, or in his presence. The people would worship the god and the other gods before him.

But the first commandment makes it very clear that God is not one of many. There are no other gods, and His people were not to look to anyone or anything else to guide or sustain their lives.

Okay, that makes sense in an Old Testament context, but we are modern people, enlightened and intelligent. We don't buy into that whole "other gods" stuff . . . or do we?

Well, the truth is, we may be unwittingly worshiping other gods. Education and position. Physical appearance. Money. Happiness. Take a minute and think about your life and the things you make sacrifices to. How about your job? Your ambition? Maybe your busy schedule? Your home and the things you have acquired? Perhaps even your church work or civic involvement? Do any of those things squeeze God out of your schedule?

Don't get me wrong. Those things are not bad in and of themselves. But have you kept them in their appropriate and proper place?

Can good, worthwhile things come before God? How does that fit with the very first and most important commandment?

I offer you no answers today . . . just the challenge to ask some questions and identify some "other gods."

> "'I am the Lord your God, who brought you out of Egypt, out of the land of slavery. You shall have no other gods before me.'" (Exodus 20:2–3)

## Struggling Continued

We all suffer painful losses. There are times when the strongest of us are so devastated by a loss that we can't see past the pain. Tomorrow doesn't exist. Grief overwhelms us and we simply can't function anymore. Any time a loss totally devastates a person and recovery doesn't seem like an option, it is a sign that our hearts are struggling with the first commandment. That sounds cruel, I know, but just keep reading.

We all struggle with idols in our lives. God says that we are to have no other gods before or beside Him. I can understand that on a religious level, but on a practical level it is more difficult. Does God really expect us to never love any person or anything as much as we love Him? Can good things become idols? Can our love for a friend or a child or a marriage partner ever be too strong? Can love of life itself or even service to God capture our heart in a way that only God Himself deserves?

Hard questions! Easy answer. Yes!

When God commands that we love Him first and most, it is for our own good that we struggle to obey. You see, the love of God will never fail. It will never leave us, never die or betray us. The love of God is eternal and sure, and if it is the primary love of our lives, it will be enough to sustain us through any situation . . . through any loss.

So, does that mean we should love the people in our lives less? Absolutely not! It means that if we intentionally spend our lives in the discipline of loving God *first*, our love for others will be of a higher quality because it flows through us, not from us. It also means that when all else fails us, we are rock solid, planted and rooted in the love that will not let us go.

O Love that wilt not let me go,
I rest my weary soul in thee;
I give thee back the life I owe,
That in thine ocean depths its flow
May richer, fuller be.
   —George Matheson

That's how it works. Give it all back to God and He will make the flow richer and fuller. Those you love will be loved better when you love God first.

> "Jesus replied: '"Love the Lord your God with all your heart and with all your soul and with all your mind." This is the first and greatest commandment. And the second is like it, "Love your neighbor as yourself."'" (Matthew 22:37–39)

## The Weakness and Strength of the Struggle

So if we have considered which people and things are most important in our lives, and if we are willing to give God's paradigm a shot—to prioritize in such a way that God alone occupies the No. 1 spot—it follows that something else is going to get knocked out of first place. What happens when putting God first bumps someone or something else down a notch on our priority ladder? Something or someone will no longer be getting most of our time or our greatest attention. This is discipline, my friends. And it might be tough!

I can bear witness to you that God is faithful to put Himself in the place of our losses. He fills any void by drawing us nearer to

Himself. Think about this. What questions and doubts come to your mind? These are the hard questions we need to embrace if we truly would be what God intends.

To tell you the truth, sometimes I'm scared of what it will cost. Does that make me sound weak? If I am brutally honest, I really love the things in my life that make me comfortable. I like to look competent and to have the respect of people. But these good things can be dangerous if I allow them to become too important. It isn't our weaknesses we need to think about letting go of; it's our strengths. Our reputation, success, health, popularity, comfort, and sometimes our friends.

Several years ago I was challenged to honor the first commandment . . . to examine my life carefully and to be willing to abandon everything that was in competition with my love for God. It was scary. I was experiencing some poor health that sapped my strength, and I knew that couldn't be God's plan, so I set out to get close to Him and get well. (Ulterior motives . . . me?) I asked Him to reveal my "other gods" so that I could deal with them and get back to serving Him with the best I had to offer.

I was in Ireland at the time and was taking a break, running laps around a rugby field and asking God to show me how to be strong enough to serve Him better. It was so strange! As I ran, a Scripture reference came to my mind. I couldn't remember what the verse said, but "2 Corinthians 12:9" kept running through my mind. I ran back into the gym and took my Bible out of my bag. But when I found the verse, I was devastated . . . and *angry*. "My grace is sufficient for you, for my power is made perfect in weakness."

"Wrong verse!" was my whole prayer of response.

My health continued to worsen, but I kept giving God my best . . . and I actually thought progress was being made. I was confident that I was dealing with things well, and informed God that I understood about being weak. I was physically weak and had learned from it. End of lesson, right? Time to get well?

Later that year, and strangely enough during another trip to Ireland and while running the same field, I was recapping my thoughts and telling God (ever so humbly!) that I had seen His strength and that it was time to heal me so I could serve well. The reply I heard in my heart was, "You don't have a clue how strong I am!"

I wanted God to heal me. He had done that before, and I believed He could again—with all my heart. It was what I wanted, but apparently not what I needed.

I tell you this because it has been the hardest lesson I've ever learned: My "other god" was *me!* God took my strength and left me only the promise that I still had His strength. Funny, that God promises to be most strong in our weakness, and yet people (even good Christian people) hate to see weakness.

That's what's on my mind today . . . the fact that we sort of wink at some of God's power, but don't really believe what He says. We look for strong, competent people to help us achieve our idea of what God wants. People run from weakness and consider those who seem weak to be of little value.

When God took away my strength, He also took away the things I had loved too much. He took me to a place where all I had left to worship was Him. Then I realized the difference between my strength and His strength. Painful? Yeah. But worth every tear!

How do we treat people who are weak? What do we do when we are weak? Who do we turn to when God seems to have removed the things that reassure us and make us feel secure? How weak is weak enough for God's strength to show up in us? Do you have the courage to think about these questions and to bring them to Him for answers?

Put Him first and rely on His strength.

> "My grace is sufficient for you, for my power is made perfect in weakness." (2 Corinthians 12:9)

## Twice Mine

A little boy spent many weeks, working hard, building a toy sailboat. Once it was finished, it was his pride and joy. One day he took it out for a sail on a lake and a gust of wind swept his toy boat away. The string that secured it snapped and he watched as his pride and joy sailed out of his reach and then out of his sight.

Several weeks later the boy passed a toy store and there was his boat in the window! The owner told him the price and the boy went home and began saving his money. He worked odd jobs and extra chores until he had the right amount of money. He bought back his prized schooner, and clutching it in his hand he said, "You are mine, *twice!* Mine because I made you, and mine because I bought you!"

The idea I'd like you to carry with you today is the picture of the boy clutching the boat in his hand. That is the definition of redemption. You belong to God twice. Remember that. You need to hear God say to you this day, as He holds you in His hand: "You are mine, *twice!* Mine because I made you, and mine because I bought you. You are my pride and joy."

> "If I rise on the wings of the dawn, if I settle on the far side of the sea, even there your hand will guide me, your right hand will hold me fast." (Psalm 139:9–10)

# The Palm Pilot and the Holy Spirit

My husband is very good to me. Whenever a new electronic gadget or tool comes on the market, he sees that it is something I really need and he buys it for me. I don't like electronic gadgets much . . . at least not until I'm forced to learn how to use them. Lucky for me he is willing to suffer through acquiring and playing with all sorts of new stuff, just for me!

When palm pilots were new, he bought me one. In theory it was a good thing for me to have. I kept it by my bed and mostly played games on it. Then my husband gave me the real gift. He spent a weekend entering the names and addresses of my friends and he put my schedule on the calendar. Suddenly the gadget had worth. It contained the memory of important things that I could retrieve when I needed them.

Which brings me to the question for today. Why is it important to keep reading the Bible? You've read the stories already. Why read them again?

The answer: Every time you read, hear, or study God's Word it's like putting information in your palm pilot. Your mind ("love the Lord your God with all your mind" . . . remember?) becomes better equipped to meet your needs and the needs of others as you program God's Word into your memory. You become better equipped for life and for worship.

As you become familiar with God's Word, that Word becomes yours, and the Holy Spirit will help you retrieve information you have stored. If you want to experience the power of the Holy Spirit as your teacher, enter as much information as you can for Him to use in your life. Remember: He can only remind you of things you have already heard.

Input the Word. Then, when situations arise that require wisdom from God's Word, the Holy Spirit, at work in you, will bring to your mind things you may not even consciously remember learning! Isn't that amazing?

> "But the Counselor, the Holy Spirit, whom the Father will send in my name, will teach you all things and will remind you of everything I have said to you.'" (John 14: 26)

## Another Palm Pilot Thought

I have a friend who writes on his hand. If he is going to meet you at certain time, or if he is going to call you, he will take out a pen and write that time or date on his hand. Eric told me once it was his "palm pilot." I've actually seen my name written on his hand, and I liked it.

God has written my name on His hand, too. Actually, He has engraved it there. I need to sit with Him and see my name on His hand . . . and remember.

Before you run off to start your busy day, read the verse below. It's a word from the One who matters. Believe it, imagine it, and remember it.

> "See, I have engraved you on the palms of my hands.'" (Isaiah 49:16)

## Thirsty

I once had a teacher who had spent time in Calcutta working with Mother Teresa in her ministry to the poor. He said that for a full hour in the morning before they went out to serve the poor they worshiped and had communion . . . every day. He said that up in the front of their chapel was a crucifix, and above Jesus' head were the words, "I thirst." Below His feet were the words, "We quench." Mother Teresa taught that serving others is really serving Jesus Himself. He thirsts; we quench His thirst through our loving, obedient service to others. That's very cool.

There are so many things about Jesus that are too hard for me to understand. But I understand giving a drink or giving a ride or being a friend. And somehow, in the world of the Spirit and the heart, that serves Jesus Himself.

God doesn't ask us to be religious. He asks us to be His friend by being friends to the people He loves.

So the question for the day is: Who are His friends and what am I doing about it? Love outside of your "group" this week. See what happens.

"He who oppresses the poor shows contempt for their Maker, but whoever is kind to the needy honors God."
(Proverbs 14:31)

## I Remember

I had the most wonderful dream last night . . . actually this morning. I dreamed I was with my little boys, Mike and Kevin (both young men now), and they were about three and six years old. They had striped shirts on that I remember them having, and they were making the same awful jokes they made back then. We were trying to build a fort out of mattresses, pillows, and blankets. We laughed and played and then I woke up completely wrapped up in the happiness of that dream. For just a few minutes I was back in a time I don't often remember with such detail. Other things were important then. Other goals filled my days. And so I'm sitting here, tears streaming, as I let God remind me of His blessings to me over the years. Joy.

Sara Groves sings a song called "Stir My Heart." It is one of my favorites. In it she asks God to bring back to her mind recollections of joy. Yeah. How very sweet to remember joy and let it stir something deep down inside.

Back when my children were little, my highest priority was someone else's happiness. I remember how my days were planned around little kindnesses and adventures that would be special to my kids. I remember how I could sit and listen to my little girl, Krista, tell me stories that took twists and turns of an amazing imagination and that made my day. I had the time to listen. I remember spending hours doing small things . . . like baking banana bread together, or carving pumpkins . . . and those things were so very important. My kids' happiness mattered. I wanted them to understand love. I wanted them to think about Jesus every day in a way that would create comfort and familiarity. I don't remember meetings or TV shows, phone calls or chores. I had time to just be with the ones I loved.

What if I still invested that much energy in other people's happiness? That felt so good! I remember! Lord, renew my first desire and help me keep the important things *first*. Help me love with all my heart, soul, mind, and strength . . . this day.

That's my prayer for you today . . . that you remember joy. Of course I hope this day brings you plenty of its own, but there is something so sweet in remembering a time when you were filled with the presence of God in a way that was a special blessing.

> "I remember the days of long ago; I meditate on all your works and consider what your hands have done. I spread out my hands to you; my soul thirsts for you like a parched land." (Psalm 143:5–6)

(Recommended listening: *Past the Wishing,* "Stir My Heart," by Sara Groves.)

## Who Are You?

My dad was really an awesome father and I loved to just hang out with him while he worked or did errands or played. I learned so much from him. Lots of people don't have that kind of relationship to draw from, but I do, and I treasure it. When my dad died, I was devastated. Actually, I was lost. It took a while, but eventually God brought me to the place where I began to let *Him* fill in for my dad. And you know what? He has. I find that spending time just listening to God . . . in the silence or in music or in His Word or in other believers . . . is amazing time for me. God Almighty wants me as His daughter! Why? I don't know, but He does.

The truth is that we are children of God . . . His very own . . . *by His choice* (1 John 3:1). And children of the heavenly Father don't need to earn love or work for acceptance. They can just hang out with their Father and get to know Him a little better each day. I am amazed at this still, even after all these years.

Let this truth sink in, okay? You are God's beloved child by His choice. You don't need to earn or buy His love and acceptance, and it's a relationship you never need to fear. He won't disappoint you or hurt you. I'm not sure why this seems so important to pass on to you today. Maybe you'll know. There's no good reason to fight that kind of love.

> "How great is the love the Father has lavished on us, that we should be called children of God!" (1 John 3:1)

## Bottom Logs

I built a fire in the fireplace the other day, with a starter log on the bottom and a nice big fat log on top of it. As the day wore on and the fire burned, I noticed that the bottom log started to turn to embers, and as I put a new log on top there were three distinct layers. The bottom log was red hot and kept the whole thing burning, the middle log had caught on pretty well, and eventually the top log became a part of a really great fire.

Made me think . . . if there is no bottom log, or if I move it out of proximity to the middle log, the fire no longer lies on red-hot embers and it dies down. The key is to keep building off the fire of the bottom log until it is consumed and the middle log becomes the bottom log. Forgive me if the analogy is corny, but isn't that how a life of faith is supposed to be? The "old" log needs to give what it has to the middle log, to help it catch fire, and then to keep it burning enough to ignite the new wood.

We each spend time in these three stages. We are new in the faith, we have a time to catch on and reach out, and then we must take our turn at being red-hot embers—giving ourselves in the cause of keeping the fire burning. If the more seasoned believers choose to retire, what does that do to the fire? When we don't make ourselves and our experiences constantly available to those who are younger, it is harder for them to take on leadership roles and to ignite the next generation.

Many mature Christians fail as bottom logs. When it comes to teaching the traditions of the faith and sharing stories of their struggles in life, either they try to set aside who they are in an effort to be "new and relevant," or they become removed and unavailable in any real way to the next generation of leaders. Worse yet, they refuse the role of support for the new middle log, whose job is to reach the new, yet unkindled wood.

Sometimes the middle logs take the mantle of leadership without valuing the wisdom of those who are older, and they see the embers as "old-fashioned" and dispensable. Is this the reason totally modern, trendy, or fad-driven faith sometimes doesn't have much staying power?

I look at the life of the apostle Paul and see how he invested himself in the next generation, like Titus and Timothy. When Paul was all used up, those he had discipled were ready to be solid, confident leaders, and they trained the next generation . . . on and on for thousands of years! Had one generation failed to pass on the faith, how would you and I have heard that there is a God, that He can be known, and that we can live in relationship with Him through the work of Jesus? We each come as the top log, spend some time as the middle, and then *must* be true to the mission of being the bottom log . . . the embers that feed the fire.

Think for a minute about the "bottom logs" in your life and thank God for them. Seek out the wisdom and friendship of older believers. They know things you need to know to keep your spiritual fire hot. Everything God brings into your life will help you burn with a purpose when it's your turn to be a bottom log.

> "[At the death of Moses] Joshua son of Nun was filled with the spirit of wisdom because Moses had laid his hands on him. So the Israelites listened to him and did what the Lord had commanded Moses." (Deuteronomy 34:9)

## Recess

It's frozen here today. My husband, Jon, and I walked the dogs this afternoon, and when they ran, I slid behind them. We stayed out until our fingers were purple and our noses red, and the dogs ran until they were about to drop. As they ran and tried to bite the falling snow I was sliding up and down ice-crusted hills . . . I felt like a ten-year-old. Jon and I talked a lot but avoided anything that required deep thought. We laughed much. Now I'm in by a fire, cheeks red, reading and preparing for a class . . . and wishing that every day brought some kind of childish release and fun like this one has. Good to be children, huh? Wish I were smart enough to take recess every day. This has been a real gift.

I believe God enjoys His children when they enjoy His creation. Like making and giving a gift to someone you love, your joy is multiplied when you watch that gift used and enjoyed. Today enjoy

God's gifts to you. Laugh out loud. Take in a huge breath and sigh it away . . . thinking about a God who desires your happiness.

> "Shout for joy to the Lord, all the earth, burst into jubilant song with music; make music to the Lord with the harp, with the harp and the sound of singing, with trumpets and the blast of the ram's horn—shout for joy before the Lord, the King." (Psalm 98:4–6)

## Growing Deep

Oswald Chambers says of the apostle Paul: "Paul is like a musician who does not need the approval of the audience if he can catch the look of approval from his Master." (*My Utmost for His Highest*)

That's what I want to be when I grow up! To be a performer, as Os Guinness has said, for an audience of One.

In the body of Christ we all have jobs to do, ways to serve God's people. It's pretty easy to do the jobs that make people happy. It's a comfortable exhaustion that yields the smiles and nods of the people we care about. The church should be a safe place to obey God's call on our lives; a place where people gather around to love, encourage, and protect us. When that's the case, obedience is pretty easy. But sometimes, especially if God has something special to teach us, it's just not that simple.

Sometimes God asks us to do things that have a cost attached. (Like the New Testament isn't full of that very warning?) There are times when obedience to God's voice in our hearts isn't the popular path to take, even within the church. That's when we realize what audience we are playing to. That's when we understand how much we try to be what others want us to be, and to serve in ways that please them. But when God takes us to a lonely place of obedience, it's important to remember that He knows what He's doing, and that when He gets us all alone, that is where He can grow us deep.

Don't be afraid, and don't pass up the opportunity for difficult obedience! If you find yourself standing alone, keep your mind and your heart and your eyes fixed on the Master. You aren't there by coincidence. He is right there with you, growing you deep. Obedience is never failure in God's eyes, even if it makes you feel like a failure. I think we do ourselves great harm by sidestepping the assignment when God asks us to speak an unpopular viewpoint or stand up for an unpopular person. If obedience is always easy, you can be sure that your walk isn't taking you any deeper into God.

God Almighty deals with each of us one-on-one. Today, try to play to Him, the audience of one . . . and remember that He is the only one who matters. Sometimes we mess up. I find a strange freedom in admitting that at times I have been a magnificent failure, but I keep trying to follow His lead and obey what He says, and I can tell you with all the confidence in the world that my messes have been of little consequence to God! He just sets me back on my feet and says "try again." That's where He grows me deep, and that's how I know He's God.

> "'Be careful not to do your "acts of righteousness" before men, to be seen by them.'" (Matthew 6:1)

## Amazing to Me

I met a young man in Colorado named Todd. God puts songs into his heart so that other people will be able to hear His voice. He helped me to hear. Today I want to give you God's words as Todd sang them right into my heart. I pray you'll hear them . . . that you'll take them personally . . . and find a way to believe them.

You've been through hell and back,
say that your life is crashed.
I know it well.
You think you're not good enough to come and talk
after everything you've done and all.
I know it well.
But push through that lie.
That is not My voice to you

I am with you.
I am not ashamed of you.
I am proud that you are My child.
I take joy in you, every unique thing you do.
You'll never ever cease to be
amazing to Me.

So come sit down with Me.
I just can't wait to hear your voice.
Cause My love is deep for you,
wide for you,
there's nothing I won't do to keep you.
Now just to see your face makes Me smile,

after everything we've been through and all,
you know it well.
So run through those lies,
run into My embrace.

For I am with you.
I am not ashamed of you.
I am proud that you are My child
I take joy in you, every unique thing you do.
You'll never, ever, ever cease to be
amazing to Me.
  (Todd Warren)

You are so loved. How long has it been since you've let yourself believe the love of God . . . with no ifs or buts? Any other message you hear is a lie. Don't settle for that.

> "For the Lord takes delight in his people; he crowns the humble with salvation. Let the saints rejoice in this honor and sing for joy on their beds." (Psalm 149:4–5)

(Recommended listening: *Honeyrock*, "Amazing," by Todd Warren. Used here by permission. See www.TODDWARREN.com)

## Finding God . . . or Maybe Being Found

I know that Jeremiah 29:11 is a favorite verse of lots of people. "'For I know the plans I have for you,' declares the Lord, 'plans to prosper you and not to harm you, plans to give you hope and a future.'" What a great thing to hear, that God has plans to prosper us. I love that! But if you stop there, you miss the best part. "'Then you will call upon me and come and pray to me, and I will listen to you.'" Amazing! God will give us His full attention! Then read the next part. "'You will seek me and find me when you seek me with all your heart. I will be found by you,' declares the Lord."

*This day*, seek Him with all your heart. Take the time you need to ask God to show Himself to you, and let that expectation grow in your thoughts as you begin your day. He will be found by you . . . *this very day*!

Wherever you are, whatever your schedule, seek Him. You may find Him at work or at lunch, in class or in traffic, on the bus or walking down the street, in a friend or in a stranger. Be watching and listening. The key is to keep seeking Him with all your heart. Be watching and listening.

Don't expect God to jump out from behind a tree or grab you by the collar. Rather, think of playing hide-and-seek as a child. If you stop seeking, you have no chance of finding. He says you will find Him if you are intent on looking. And when you find Him, stop right there and have a little worship.

This could be a seriously wonder-filled day.

> "'You will seek me and find me when you seek me with all your heart. I will be found by you.'" (Jeremiah 29:13)

## Whatever You've Got

I read something a couple of days ago and it's still rattling around in my head. "Worship is giving God the best that He has given you. Be careful what you do with the best you have" (Oswald Chambers, *My Utmost for His Highest*).

God has given me a unique friendship with a brother who shares my heart for Jesus as few others do. We have worked together for years and have shared a common quest to give the things that God has given us . . . very "unspiritual" things sometimes . . . back to Him, trusting that He has not made us as we are randomly. The thought of giving talents and abilities, time and care, in very worldly settings seems like what Jesus had in mind when He told His followers to "go into the world . . . "

This friend and I met for breakfast and prayer the other day, and as I drove home it hit me why time spent with him always fills me up. Plotting and planning ways to give our best to God is worship! I worshiped today over coffee and very bad oatmeal . . . talking about hundreds of kids and basketball.

What natural skills and abilities has God put in you as standard equipment? What drives you? Be intentional about giving it back to Him and you will experience worship! Does that make sense? Man, it does to me. Today I am filled. Today I have worshiped God.

Be careful what you do with the best you have.

"Therefore, I urge you, brothers, in view of God's mercy, to offer your bodies as living sacrifices, holy and pleasing to God—this is your spiritual act of worship." (Romans 12:1)

# Worship

My mind has been coming back to thoughts about worship all week! Here's what I'm thinking. When God measures our lives, He won't see what we have built or what we have accomplished . . . only how well we have worshiped.

I was created to worship God. My accomplishments and the things I build in this life can all be taken away or ruined by circumstances or by other people. But my worship of God cannot be touched by anyone except God and me. It's personal. It is how well I learn to relate to the One who made me, for the purpose He made me.

The most perfect worship is taking everything God has given us and finding ways to give it back to Him. It's how we love and teach and serve.

It's easy to go to church and be led into worship (and that's a wonderful thing), but what about the rest of my life? How do I handle conversations to the glory of God? How do I use my home, use my phone, use my "stuff" for the glory of God? How do I work and learn and think to the glory of God?

Whatever you were planning to do right after you read this, how can you do it to the glory of God?

Don't you just love a challenge?

Walk well today. Worship as you walk. It's good for you.

> "Do not conform any longer to the pattern of this world, but be transformed by the renewing of your mind. Then you will be able to test and approve what God's will is—his good, pleasing and perfect will." (Romans 12:2)

# Maggie

Sometimes when I wake in the morning I have the feeling that someone is watching me. Have you ever had that feeling? I sleep on my right side, so all I have to do is open one eye to check and see if my guardian angel is there . . . and she always is.

Maggie is 112 pounds of sweetness wrapped up in a yellow lab. She has a remarkable sense of knowing when someone needs her . . . unlike her brother Jake (a chocolate lab), who only has a sense of knowing when someone has food. Maggie comes and stands by my bed with her chin resting right next to my pillow. She just stands there and looks. She breathes through her nose, so she is totally silent. You only get this feeling that someone is there. Sometimes she stands there for a really long time. When I open my eyes and she sees that I see her, she still just stands there wagging her tail.

You know that God has revealed Himself through creation, right? Well, He has taught me about faithfulness and friendship through this one part of His creation called Maggie. All she does is stand there, but it reminds me every single morning that even before I wake there is Someone watching and waiting for me. It's easy for me to remember that Maggie is there. I can see her. Her purpose, I think, is to remind me of what I can't see.

Remember the faithfulness of the ever-present, watching and waiting Father . . . closer to you than your breath. And remember to stand by your friends. Sometimes just your presence in their life is enough to remind them of what they can't see.

"I will never leave you or forsake you," God said to Joshua. That's one promise we can take for ourselves and also pass on to our friends.

Dogs are faithful! People . . . well, we need a push now and then.

"'No one will be able to stand up against you all the days of your life. As I was with Moses, so I will be with you; I will never leave you nor forsake you.'" (Joshua 1:5)

## The Right Use of a Heart

What happens when a person gives his heart away? It means he has agreed to share emotions with another person. He opens himself up to be loved, and he opens himself up to the possibility of being hurt. Joy and sorrow are multiplied when we choose to love.

Giving your heart to Jesus means you have given control of its use over to Him. If I have really given my heart to Him, I have agreed to share in His love for other people—and He really loves a lot of people (even people who don't love back). That's just part of the deal I guess. God doesn't ask me to choose whom I will love. He just keeps breaking and remaking my heart . . . a bit bigger each time to accommodate more of His beloved children. Giving my heart to Jesus doesn't just mean that He will *save* me. It means that I have agreed to let Him *use* my heart as He sees fit. Yow!

That's a nice thought; letting God use my heart, right? But I am just not that loving! Face it, sometimes I find it hard to even like people! I don't have a big enough heart or enough love. But if God's Word is true, it seems the more I give, the more there will be to give. Check this out: "'Give, and it will be given to you. A good measure, pressed down, shaken together and running over, will be poured into your lap. For with the measure you use, it will be measured to you'" (Luke 6:38).

Have you ever measured brown sugar in a cup? You have to press it down and pack the cup full to get the correct amount. That's what I picture with these words of Jesus. Give your heart to Him, and He will begin to pack it full of people to love. Give your heart to those He loves, and your supply of love will overflow. There is no end to it! Keep giving, and *He* will give back to you. More than you ever imagined!

Today I'm thinking about those people I have come to love because I just can't help it. I didn't set out to love them! But God brought them into my life, and as I prayed for them, He found space in my heart for just one more. I'm thinking of how rich I have become by giving away God's love, and how amazed I am when the love comes back to me. Some days it's almost more than I can handle! Only God could think up a plan like this.

Love somebody today. Not because you really want to, or because they are loveable, but because you've given God control of your heart. This is one of those things you've got to experience before you know it's true. Try it.

> "'Do to others as you would have them do to you. If you love those who love you, what credit is that to you? Even 'sinners' love those who love them . . . Give and it will be given to you. . . .'" (Luke 6:31–33, 38)

## I Dare You

I have a challenge for you and I wonder if you can do it. I wonder if anybody can. It involves discipline . . . one of your favorite words, I know! Anyway, it's worth trying.

We live in a world of people who are killing each other in the name of peace. "Peace at any price!" scream angry people with clenched fists. We are an agitated lot! Road rage, riots, fights, pressures of money and work . . . there is little evidence of peace in people's hearts. But there is a way to find peace. In fact, it's a promise: "Finally, my brothers, whatever is true, whatever is noble, whatever is right, whatever is pure, whatever is lovely, whatever is admirable—if anything is excellent or praiseworthy—think about such things. Whatever you have learned or received or heard from me, or seen in me—put it into practice. And the God of peace will be with you" (Philippians 4:8–9).

This is one of those passages that might be overlooked or put in the "nice thought for today" category, but read it again. This is hard stuff! Peace doesn't come easily, because it comes through the discipline of our minds. I'll bet you can't do what this verse says for even a day . . . no, make that a quarter of a day. What am I saying! I'll bet you can't do it for two hours. We're talking about some serious effort here. Really, how can anyone control every thought? It's nearly impossible to avoid all the junk and smut—it's everywhere.

Here's the challenge. Isolate yourself for just a little while and seriously exercise control over your thoughts. Refuse bad humor and tragic news. Do not allow cruel movies or stories or lyrics to touch your mind, and watch out for newspapers and magazines . . . just for a little while. Choose not to listen . . . not to look. No gossip, no listening to bad things said about someone else, no thoughts of hate or revenge. You will be amazed at how much ungodly stuff surrounds you and fills your thoughts. No wonder you're exhausted and have no peace!

Put yourself on a fast from filth for, say, eight hours, and see what the space in your brain and your heart fills itself with! (And the eight hours while you're sleeping don't count.)

I'm dead serious. Do it as an experiment . . . as a gift to yourself and to God. Pray first. Then find an eight-hour chunk of time this week and set it aside. "Too busy" isn't a valid excuse. People give up chocolate and candy and meat for Lent. Wouldn't God rather have us give up filth?

An eight-hour fast from filth. Hmm. Why is that so tough?

> "And the God of peace will be with you." If you want . . . if you dare. . . . (Philippians 4:8–9)

## Eating and Breathing

My thoughts lately have been about holiness. I love it. I want it. But what is it?

> "Our progress in holiness depends on God and ourselves—on God's grace and on our will to be holy."
> —Mother Teresa

> "[Holiness] evidences itself in the decisions we make and the things we do, hour by hour, day by day."
> —Chuck Colson

I gather from these two statements that holiness is something I need to set my mind (my will) toward, and as I become holy it will be evident in the things I do and the decisions I make. The only way I can experience holiness in my life is to set my conscious decision-making mind toward the total control of God's Holy Spirit living in me. I cannot accomplish holiness by hard work. I cannot accomplish it by choosing to act in holy ways. Only God can make me holy, and He will never do that if it goes against my will.

"Be holy, because I am holy," says the Lord (Leviticus 11:45). "Be perfect, therefore as your heavenly Father is perfect," says Jesus (Matthew 5:48). Don't *do* holy or *act* holy. *Be* holy. The evidence that shows the saturating presence of God and His Word in someone's life will make itself obvious in holiness. That's a large thought . . . take a minute to think it through carefully.

Sunday in church we sang the song "Breathe," written by Michael W. Smith. Do you know that one? The song speaks of God's presence in the air we breathe and His Word as the daily bread that nourishes us. The song lingers in the back of my mind today, constantly reminding me that the indwelling Holy Spirit of God needs to be the condition in which I live—I need it every bit as much as I need oxygen and calories. (I would soon notice if either of those elements were missing!)

Think about that. God's holy presence . . . living in me . . . would make me holy, right? So I need to pay attention to the air I breathe—to keep myself in an atmosphere that is indeed the presence of God. And how do I keep myself strong enough to seek out this right atmosphere? Well, eating right is essential—and that means God's holy Word, my daily bread, spoken to me. I can't seek out good air when I'm starving . . . can't find good food if I'm suffocating. This means there is no way any of us can ignore God or His Word. Without food or air we can't expect to make it through the day.

What are you doing for the next ten minutes? Just take a bit of time to nourish yourself. Then set out to breathe deeply of God all day. You will be better equipped for this day and all the stuff packed into your schedule (especially if Satan has planned some surprises for you).

I pray that you will desire to seek what is good this day so your actions and reactions will be amazingly holy.

"Anyone who lives on milk, being still an infant, is not acquainted with the teaching about righteousness. But solid food is for the mature, who by constant use have trained themselves to distinguish good from evil." (Hebrews 5:13–14)

(Recommended listening: *Creation Worships*, "Breathe," by Michael W. Smith, sung by Rita Springer.)

## Wordless Prayer

As I set out to begin this morning in prayer I sit by my office window, just looking out on a beautiful day. I see a great blue heron standing knee-deep in the lake and seagulls flying overhead. There are men digging up a tree and men hitting golf balls. And I wonder why the dead leaves still cling to that oak tree when the maples stand completely bare. I see two jet streams making an X in the blue sky and a Frisbee in the backyard. Sirens somewhere down the road make me wonder about who is about to be helped . . . or caught. Somebody is burning leaves . . . I can smell it. My coffee is hot and steamy and my mind seems to be wandering in hyper-drive today. I am momentarily upset with myself that I can't seem to just close my eyes and pray this morning . . . and then I read Henri Nouwen's words and have an "ah ha!" moment.

> When we walk in the Lord's presence, everything we see, hear, touch, or taste reminds us of him. This is what is meant by a prayerful life. It is not a life in which we say many prayers, but a life in which nothing, absolutely

nothing is done, said or understood independently of him who is the origin and purpose of our existence.

—Henri J. Nouwen

This is like visiting an art gallery of masterpieces or being surrounded by the sounds of a symphony. I am left with my mouth gaping and speechless at the sight of creation around me. I don't critique what I see, nor would I think of explaining it to the Artist. Sometimes prayer has nothing to do with words or explanations. It's just noticing things . . . noticing God . . . in everything. This is overwhelming prayer.

A candle sputters on my desk and brings my mind back inside. The flame reminds me of Pentecost. "Oh my God!" are the only words I can find. And tears.

I know so little. Perhaps this is why "Hallmark" Christianity is so very offensive to me. It sums up everything, makes faith definable and cute. No open-ended wonder. No open-eyed awe. What I am breathing in and out in prayer this morning could never be a cute saying on a coffee mug or a T-shirt.

How sad to try to make God cute, to reduce Him to a clever saying, when we could be looking around in wide-eyed wonder, aware that His presence fills and surrounds all of our senses.

I pray for you today, my friends, a wordless prayer. He is your breath . . . your beating heart. Notice.

"O Lord, our Lord, how majestic is your name in all the earth! . . . When I consider your heavens, the work of your fingers, the moon and the stars, which you have set in place . . . " and the rest of Psalm 8. (Psalm 8)

# How to Fly

Have you ever had one of those weeks that just takes everything you have and leaves you exhausted? Well, I just had one. Sometimes it's your job that does it to you. Sometimes it's a person you deal with or a challenging situation.

I was writing in my journal and trying to put the past few days into words, and I realized something . . . I'm a better person than I was a week ago, I think—a bit stronger, a bit more peaceful. How did that happen?

This past week things happened that required me to think long and hard before acting . . . to see things from another perspective . . . to extend an understanding attitude and a forgiving heart . . . to ask forgiveness for my own insensitivity. That's work. I didn't enjoy it. But apparently I needed it.

I wonder, will learning and growing ever get easier? Will I ever get to the point where I know enough . . . where there's no more to learn? I wish.

I just read something that made me laugh. Here it is, from C. S. Lewis: "It may be hard for an egg to turn into a bird, but it would be a jolly sight harder for it to learn to fly while remaining an egg."

As I pray for you today I don't have any idea what sort of week you've had, but there is one thing I do know: There isn't anything that comes into your day that won't make you a better person if you pay attention and ask God to teach you through it.

When things are challenging, you can be sure the exercise is designed specifically for the purpose of moving you one step closer to being who you were created to be . . . and to fly.

Always one more thing to learn, it would seem.

Nothing is wasted.

"Not only so, but we also rejoice in our sufferings, because
we know that suffering produces perseverance;
perseverance, character; and character, hope. And hope
does not disappoint us, because God has poured out his love
into our hearts by the Holy Spirit, whom he has given us."
(Romans 5:3–5)

## Jam Today!

A little thought from Lewis Carroll's *Alice's Adventures in Wonderland*:

> "The rule is, jam tomorrow, and jam yesterday—but
> never jam today."
> "It must come sometimes to 'jam today,'" Alice
> objected.
> "No it can't," said the Queen. "It's jam every other
> day: today isn't every other day, you know."

I am here to tell you that the Queen is wrong! We are always
worried about what we have done or what we need to do. There is
always someone who wants us to perform in one way or another.
True? Well, guess what? Today is jam!

It was a big deal to Jesus that we live today, in the moment.
That's why forgiveness is so important. There is nothing to clean
up or prove when God forgives us. We are clean, set, ready to take
on the present. And tomorrow will only be better if today is done
well. So, live today well.

Really live your life today, whatever your circumstance. Use
your faith to let you enjoy the presence of God. It's what He wants.

If you feel you need permission of some sort to enjoy your life today, read Matthew 6:25–34. At the very least, stop here and now and invite your Lord into your day!

Jam today! Eat lots. Let it make you sticky and sweet all over. Share it with a stingy and hungry world. Jam today can only make the difficult more palatable, the ordinary more extraordinary, and the good better.

It's okay for you to enjoy this day.

> "'Therefore do not worry about tomorrow, for tomorrow will worry about itself. Each day has enough trouble of its own.'" (Matthew 6:34)

## Good Company

Around the turn of the twentieth century, Hannah Johanesson left Sweden to come to America. She traveled by herself on a boat full of strangers heading to a strange land. The people who were supposed to meet her in New York didn't show up, so at the age of thirteen, speaking only Swedish, Hannah began to make a new life on her own. Somehow she found her way, and somewhere along the way, she met Jesus. She wasn't one for sentimentality, she wasn't interested in "doing religion," but she adored Jesus. She counted on Him. He was the most real thing in her life. When she spoke His name it was with tenderness and wonder.

I don't know why I'm thinking about her today. Maybe because of the testimony of her life. Or maybe because Jesus hasn't changed since then and I want to remind myself that He is faithful to me just as He was faithful to my grandma all those years ago.

My grandma's belief in His faithfulness is reflected in her favorite hymn, written by Joseph Scriven in 1855. As a young man, Scriven became estranged from his family because of his faith in Jesus. Then, the night before his wedding, his fiancée drowned. At age twenty-five Scriven left his home in Dublin, Ireland, and, like my grandma, never returned to his homeland again. Ten years later, when he received word that his mother was dying, he wrote these words of comfort and sent them to her.

What a Friend we have in Jesus,
All our sins and griefs to bear!
What a privilege to carry
Everything to God in prayer!
O what peace we often forfeit,
O what needless pain we bear,
All because we do not carry
Everything to God in prayer!

Sometimes it's good for me to remember that God is not bound by time. He is the same today as He was for my grandma and for Joseph Scriven, the same as He was for John the Baptist, the same as He was for Moses, the same as He was in the beginning. And we can walk and talk with Him!

The very same Jesus who helped my grandma find her way is waiting to walk each step of my life with me. I wonder, do I forfeit my peace and bear needless pain just because I forget He's there? This is a good day to remember.

"Whether you turn to the right or to the left, your ears will hear a voice behind you, saying, 'This is the way; walk in it.'" (Isaiah 30:21)

113

## Power Outages

I was just looking at a satellite photograph of the United States from the night the power blackout hit the East Coast in 2003. It is really amazing! You can see the outlines of the United States and Canada and the islands to the southeast. But the big chunk of land where New York, New Jersey, Pennsylvania, and surrounding states should be is missing. Like some celestially hungry mouth took a chunk out of that part of the earth with one big bite.

Thanks to satellite technology we can get a pretty accurate picture of where Thomas Edison has impacted the world. Wouldn't it be awesome to be able to see in the same graphic way where Jesus has impacted the world? Would we be amazed, happy, or alarmed to see our familiar world with eyes that would reveal areas of spiritual blackout? I wonder if the United States would be as well-lit by Jesus as it is by Edison. And I wonder if all the areas we assume are taken care of are really operating under another power source altogether. Are all the blacked-out areas where we think they are? How many little points of light does it take in one area to register a blip on the map?

I've been places where I could almost feel the darkness . . . the absence of God is a cold and clammy thing. Some days I'll admit I don't even think about my immediate area as being power-deprived. There are just so many churches here and so many good, busy people.

I've been reading a lot lately about spiritual warfare, and that sense of complacency is exactly what Satan wants us to have. And so today my prayer is that God would open the eyes of my heart . . . and of your heart . . . to the realities of spiritual power and spiritual power outages.

Walk well. Go light somebody up.

> "'You are the light of the world. A city on a hill cannot be hidden . . . . let your light shine before men, that they may see your good deeds and praise your Father in heaven.'" (Matthew 5:14–16; read also Ephesians 1:18–21)

## Theology of Stain Removal

We most definitely were born with a heart defect . . . thank you, Adam. The best understanding I have is that in its original condition, the heart is unable to make the right choice. Our inability to choose God has been handed down to us from Eden.

Jesus, however, purchased us a new heart. If anyone is in Christ, he is a *new creation* . . . the old has gone, the new has come (2 Corinthians 5:17). But because we live in this in-between time, when the kingdom has already come but is not totally operational yet, we must survive in this sinful world . . . with our new hearts. And because we are free in Christ, we are free to choose Him and totally defeat Satan. But the atmosphere around us is just plain toxic, and we are still human, so we still choose badly at times, even with our new hearts.

Have you seen the commercials for the new Dockers pants with stain guard? I have a pair, and it's really remarkable! I spill on them, but because the fabric has been treated, a simple washing takes the stain away. Clumsy analogy? I rather like it.

Remember when Jesus told Peter that he was clean, but his feet needed washing? Same thing, I think. Your saved, redeemed, eternal heart was transplanted upon request at Jesus' expense, and it is good. You can make it dirty, but you can't make it bad. Do you still spill on it? Yup. But thanks be to God, the stains don't stick.

That's my theology of stain removal.

> "Who will rescue me from this body of death? Thanks be to God—through Jesus Christ our Lord!" (Romans 7:24–25)

## Aslan

Today a little something from *The Chronicles of Narnia.*

"Welcome, child," he said.
"Aslan," said Lucy, "you're getting bigger."
"That is because you are older, little one," answered he.
"Not because you are?"
"I am not. But every year you grow, you will find me bigger." (*Prince Caspian*)

That's how it's supposed to be. When I was little, I had God all figured out. I knew what He looked like, where He was, and exactly what He wanted from a good little girl like me. He was bigger than me . . . but I could still fit Him into my church. Now, as I've grown and studied, listened and prayed and read, He has become so much more.

If you can find a few minutes today, see how big God is now in comparison to when you were a kid. Is He the same as He was then, or has He magnified in power and size? This will tell you how much you've grown.

Walk well today.

> "Like newborn babies, crave pure spiritual milk, so that
> by it you may grow up in your salvation, now that you
> have tasted that the Lord is good." (1 Peter 2:2–3a)

## Choose

It's early and there is no sign of sunshine this morning. It's totally gray so far. But I know the sun is there somewhere. It's morning again.

As I sit here with my coffee and my computer, I think, *This could be a wonderful day.* My mind has already touched the thoughts of God. His promises and His hope seem true at this early hour. And yet Satan is at work already, tempting my thoughts and suggesting things I may fear. Doesn't he ever take a break? I mean, it's only slightly light outside and the battle has already begun . . . and I have my first choice of the morning staring me in the face. "If serving the Lord seems undesirable to you, then choose for yourselves this day whom you will serve . . . But as for me and my household, we will serve the Lord" (Joshua 24:15).

What will it mean to choose this day to serve the Lord? Think about it. Most of the time we are satisfied to remember that, "Yes, I love God. I even became a Christian back in . . . " whenever. But this isn't about that. I'm not asking if you are eventually going to end up

117

in heaven. I'm wondering *this* day . . . right now . . . who will be in charge of you? Who will you run your decisions by? Whose voice will you listen to for direction? And if you say that this day you will serve the Lord, what difference will that make? How will that fit into your busy life?

Maybe thoughts of God should wait until you slow down and find some quiet time . . . an hour or two to give to Him in study or prayer. Nope. Bad idea. No putting this off. I love the quote from Martin Luther, "This day is so busy that I must spend three hours in prayer to prepare for it" (not an exact quote, but close enough).

Choose *this* day whom you will serve, and let God be God of the details . . . not just God of a few "sacred" moments now and then.

How amazing is it that God Almighty *wants* to be involved with organizing your schedule and handling the little things!

> "'Choose for yourselves this day whom you will serve. . . .'" (Joshua 24:15)

## Pastors

What in the world makes someone go into the ministry?

Some people seem to be born for ministry. They have a career plan and tons of ideas and objectives; they have natural gifts for that role and it's something they've wanted their whole lives. God uses people like that.

Then there are those whose lives have been interrupted by God's call, and the cost to them and their family is high. They had other plans, but God has asked them to set everything aside and follow

Him into the unknown. It's like some have enlisted and others have been drafted.

Yet all of these folks face Satan on a regular basis and are often discouraged, frequently by people they are trying to serve. They are called to demonstrate love, grace, and confidence in God, but often they fight fear and insecurities all along the way.

True pastors must love and value each person God sends their way, regardless of whether that love is returned. There is no choosing whom they are to love. God doesn't do market analysis and target groups. There are no unimportant members of the body of Christ.

So pray for the pastors in your life today. They aren't some breed of super-human; they are your fellow believers . . . most of them just trying to be faithful on a daily basis. Pray for them. And if God leads, take a minute and tell them that you are praying. Ask how you can minister to them. Don't judge their circumstances or the difficulties they may face. The wounded pastors I know have become more like Christ in their hearts and ministries as a result of their own struggles.

Good pastoring doesn't come easy. Those who are serious about becoming like Christ and serving the body will be hurt, rejected, beaten up, slandered and judged . . . just like Jesus. Don't feel sorry for them! It's part of becoming. But also don't neglect to love them and pray for them. Remember, they are precious in God's sight.

> "How beautiful on the mountains are the feet of those who bring good news, who proclaim peace, who bring good tidings, who proclaim salvation, who say to Zion, 'Your God reigns!'" (Isaiah 52:7)

## Pastoring as a Gift

Building on yesterday's call to pray for the pastors in your life, today identify those pastors in your life who work outside the church.

The whole idea of a pastor being someone who is called to a vocation, a position, and a paycheck is a relatively modern and (I believe) limited and not totally correct picture. We don't find one instance in the New Testament where a person is called to a paid position for the sake of Christ. There are no promises of financial rewards or employment, and the whole idea of prestige is foreign to the gospel. Paul does mention that someone who preaches the gospel has the right to accept the support of believers, but then goes on to say that he himself earned his own way as a tent maker.

Don't misunderstand me here . . . it's a real luxury and blessing for a church to be able to hire someone to serve as pastor, and it is an honorable calling and vocation. But there are other folks who have been given the gift of pastoring and who feel the specific call of God on their lives to develop and use their gift, but who do not enjoy the title or salary of a vocational pastor.

Once you start looking, you might be astounded to see how many pastors have influenced your life!

What is a pastor, anyway? The only time the word is used in the NIV translation of the Bible is in Ephesians 4:11. "It was he who gave some to be . . . pastors and teachers. . . ." Pastoring is a gift God gives to some so that they may serve as an integral part of the work of the body of Christ. They build it up, walk alongside the believers and help them grow toward maturity in Christ.

Take a minute and think outside your own short list of professional pastors. Is there someone who has taken time to share the wisdom of God's Word with you and has stood beside you as you struggle and grow in Christ?

In today's megachurch culture, many people will think of their pastor as the person they hear preach on Sundays, even though that pastor may not recognize them or know their name. A pastor of a thousand-member congregation just can't know everyone or stand beside them as a spiritual mentor. But God always provides other pastors to care for the members of the body. Identify them, acknowledge them as a gift from God, and support them with your prayers.

> "It was he who gave some to be apostles, some to
> be prophets, some to be evangelists, and some to
> be pastors and teachers, to prepare God's people for works
> of service, so that the body of Christ may
> be built up . . . and become mature, attaining to
> the whole measure of the fullness of Christ." (Ephesians 4:11–13)

## Cookies!

"A balanced diet is a cookie in each hand." (Sorry, it's the most inspired I've been all day—but wait, there's more.)

When I first began setting aside a Sabbath time in my life, I sought God's heart as to what would be a pleasing way for me to honor Him. I read and wrote in my journal. I sang from my old hymnal and listened to good music. I waited in silence. Some days I was so aware of the Spirit of God that I learned many great and amazing things . . . through His Word, through people He sent to me or people who called with a word of insight or encouragement. If you don't observe a Sabbath—one of the Ten Commandments you'll find in Exodus 20—then you are missing out on an incredibly important event God intends for your life! (More about that on another day.)

Today I want to tell you one thing about God that totally surprised me on my Sabbath days. One activity in which I find remarkable release and companionship with God is baking cookies! I crank up the music, get out the ingredients, sing and dance around like a mad woman as my house fills with the fragrance of a wonderful chocolate chip offering. Is that crazy? I don't think so, and here's why. All too often in my busy life I forego the treats and the special touches so that I might accomplish more weighty goals. Yet I believe it is God's good pleasure for me to sometimes just bask in His almighty presence and enjoy Him. One way to do this is to take time for the simple pleasures He affords.

Why do we find guilt in God-given pleasures? That's not His idea. Don't cut Him out of your enjoyment of life's desserts! Have you never noticed that the God of the Old Testament commanded and enjoyed good gifts of food?

Eat! Enjoy! And make enough to share in the name of the One who supplies. The joy of the Lord is our strength!

Read Nehemiah 8:5–12.

"Then Nehemiah . . . said to them all, 'This day is sacred to the Lord your God. Do not mourn or weep.' For all the people had been weeping as they listened to the words of the Law. Nehemiah said, 'Go and enjoy choice food and sweet drinks, and send some to those who have nothing prepared. This day is sacred to our Lord. Do not grieve, for the joy of the Lord is your strength.'" (Nehemiah 8:9–10)

# The Least of These

Matthew 25:31–40 is something you should take five minutes to read today. I did. Seriously, take a minute and look it up.

Often when we think of helping the homeless or the down-and-out, we think about reaching out *in the name of* Jesus *with the love of Jesus*. That's very cool. We have the amazing privilege of representing Jesus to people who have hurts and needs in this messed-up world. But that's not exactly what this passage says. Jesus doesn't say that when we visit the prisoner we are visiting in Jesus' name. No, He says when we are visiting the prisoner we are visiting JESUS!

Chris Rice has a great song in which he sings about looking into the eyes of people on the street and getting the feeling that it is Jesus who looks back at him. I wonder what kind of face you will be looking into when you recognize the eyes of Jesus looking back! Cool thought . . . a little scary.

Today, watch people. Look into their eyes. Whatever you can do for one of them is a kindness done to Jesus Himself . . . He said so.

Determine now to walk through this day with your eyes wide open, very much aware of the true identity of the "least of these" (v. 40). This kind of attitude should have us noticing people in need and reaching out with the same kind of compassionate reverence we would have for Jesus Himself.

> "'The King will reply, "I tell you the truth, whatever you did for one of the least of these brothers of mine, you did for me."'" (Matthew 25:40)

(Recommended listening: *Smell the Color of Nine*, "The Face of Christ," by Chris Rice.)

## The Flip Side

A while back there was a story in the news about a woman who left a bar one night to drive home while she was impaired. Suddenly, out of nowhere, a homeless man walked into the road and the woman hit him. He flew up and was caught in her broken windshield. The woman thought through her options. If she called for help there would be consequences she didn't want to face, so she carefully drove home with the man still on her car. She pulled her car into the garage and closed the door.

She didn't intend to harm anyone! She certainly didn't want to hurt the man, and she was very sorry, so she walked around to the front of her car and looked at the man. He was still alive and he pleaded with her to please get help. She was so sorry, she said. She apologized to the man and then went inside her house to think about the dilemma. She didn't call 911.

The woman shared the problem with friends who came and saw the man in the garage. They all expressed their sorrow to him, but there would be consequences if they involved the authorities, so they didn't call for help. After a while, the man died. Later, the coroner determined that the man would have recovered if only someone had called for help.

Of course we are all disgusted at such behavior. It seems fitting that the woman got a fifteen-year jail sentence! But do you know why she was found guilty? Not because she accidentally hit the man. Not because she was driving while impaired. She was found guilty because someone was hurt and she did nothing.

It would be okay with me if Matthew 25:40, which we read yesterday, was the end of Jesus' story about what the King will say when we are all gathered before Him. But the story continues. Take a minute and read Matthew 25:41–46. Whoa! It's not just the identity of the ones we help that we must notice, but those whom we chose to avoid and ignore.

Today, think about the people who are easy to overlook. So many needy, hurt, and dying people fill our world . . . how can we respond to them all? Maybe the question is: How can you respond to one?

> "'He will reply, "I tell you the truth, whatever you did not do for one of the least of these, you did not do for me."'"
> (Matthew 25:45)

## It's Not My Fault, Not My Business

The last two days we've been focusing on seeing the face of Christ in the individuals who fill our world. Today I want you to think in a smaller circle. Think of the people in your office, your school, your church, maybe in your own home.

Remember the woman's friends who came and saw the man on the windshield but were afraid to bring consequences down upon their friend? They did her no favor. Real friends would have loved her enough to do the right thing. Even if it brought immediate pain, it would have made the difference between an accident and a homicide. Whatever the circumstances, it just isn't a good idea to look the other way and leave someone hurting.

Have you ever seen someone hurt, maybe by gossip or exclusion by a group of people? Perhaps the ones who did the hurting were your friends, so you chose to stay uninvolved. You decided to ignore—not to see—the hurting. After all, nobody intended to cause harm! You felt sorry for the person, but confronting your friends would bring consequences you'd rather not face, so you walked away. Think about it. We've all been there.

In my opinion the friends in yesterday's story were as responsible for the death of the man as the woman behind the wheel. Will God hold us responsible for the sins of others if we choose to condone those sins by our inaction?

Wrestle with this question today so you will know what your answer is before you find yourself in one of these tough situations. Is there someone you need to talk to? Is there something you should do that you have not done? Something you need "to see" that you have ignored? Ask God to teach you something new today, and then be ready to act when He brings somebody to your mind.

"Anyone, then, who knows the good he ought to do and doesn't do it, sins." (James 4:17)

### Ah Ha!

Jesus told His friends that the Holy Spirit would remind them of all they had seen and heard from Him. The psalmist says that we are not to worry or fret, but to wait patiently for the Lord (Psalm 37:7). Faith is believing enough to wait for God to make things make sense. Confident faith dares to believe that nothing we experience will be wasted. None of it.

Aleksandr Solzhenitsyn said that life is lived forward but understood backward. Make up your mind today to keep going forward, eyes open, and believe God will make it all make sense in His time. Each joy and each hurt will one day have a profound meaning if you leave it in God's hand.

Our job is not to rush around fixing things. Our job is to wait, to watch, to trust, and then to experience the "ah ha!" of understanding Almighty God's hand in our circumstances.

Walking with God is a bit like surfing. You need to just navigate in the circumstances around you, sometimes perhaps feeling a bit out of control, but knowing that you don't control the wave . . . you just ride it. So with life, we don't absolutely control our circumstances. Far from it. Often we learn the skills we need to survive as we go. A dear friend of mine, Stephen Sharp, has written a song called "One Step at a Time," that explains this walk of faith very well. He says, "Step by step, day by day, learn to live along the way." Yeah, you learn as it's happening, and only later when you look back can you see where you've been and how it has prepared you for where you are going.

Read all of Proverbs 2, noting especially verses 5–6, 9–10:

"Then you will understand the fear of the Lord and find the knowledge of God. For the Lord gives wisdom, and from his mouth come knowledge and understanding. . . . Then you will understand what is right and just and fair— every good path. For wisdom will enter your heart, and knowledge will be pleasant to your soul."

(Recommended listening: "One Step at a Time," by Stephen Sharp.)

## Duplicate Love

I think that if I had a perfect day, it would have to include somebody who loved me enough to listen. Not compete or correct . . . just listen.

Jesus was a good listener. If you look at Scripture, again and again He asks people to tell Him what's going on. That's one way you can spot someone who is becoming like Christ . . . not that they can talk, but that they can listen.

So often things we experience don't make sense until we hear ourselves tell someone else. That's what friends do. They take the time to listen. And they help us listen to ourselves. We each have the chance to serve people in a Christlike way just by listening better.

Last night God sent me somebody who loves me . . . who has for a long time . . . and who just filled my heart with His presence in my home. Today He sent me someone else who didn't have a clue she would bring such healing to my heart. But then God usually is strongest when we are clueless, but obedient.

And so I plead with you not only to seek out someone to listen to you, but someone who might just melt if you take the time to ask how he or she is doing. I am so enormously blessed this day . . . this love needs to be duplicated.

Freely you have received, freely give. No excuses. Get out there in Jesus' name and make a difference before you go to bed tonight.

> Words of instruction to the disciples the first time Jesus sent them out to minister in His name: "'Heal the sick, raise the dead, cleanse those who have leprosy, drive out demons. Freely you have received, freely give.'" (Matthew 10:8)

## Insulin and Insolence

When my son was nineteen years old, without warning, his body ceased to provide adequate insulin and he became a Type 1 diabetic. Suddenly he needed to pay close attention to things he had given little thought to before, like what he ate and drank. Some of the things he loved were no longer an option. They would make him sick—maybe even threaten his life. He still loves the foods he loved before. He still craves a taste of his favorites and misses the comfort foods he used to enjoy, but he has learned to be careful and to discern which things will do him good and which will do him harm. There is a lesson to be learned from such discernment.

If we are living our lives for Jesus, some things, some events, and even some people just aren't good for us anymore. We still love them, and we remember fondly the comfort of old ways and old friends. But God would have us pay close attention to the things we allow into our daily diet. He would have us discern which things will do us good and which things consistently do us harm—things that take our focus off of Him.

Keeping spiritually healthy requires a disciplined diet. Pay attention to what you allow into your life.

> "But mark this: There will be terrible times in the last days. People will be lovers of themselves, lovers of money, boastful, proud, abusive, disobedient to their parents, ungrateful, unholy, without love, unforgiving, slanderous, without self-control, brutal, not lovers of the good, treacherous, rash, conceited, lovers of pleasure rather than lovers of God—having a form of godliness but denying its power. *Have nothing to do with them.*"
> (2 Timothy 3:1–5, emphasis added)

## Listen!

I've been thinking a lot about the communication I have with God, and here's what I notice. I read. I listen to music and sermons. I do church work. So most of what I think of as communication with God is actually words from an author, a songwriter, a preacher, a committee—or, from me! Yet if I truly desire communication with God, I must make sure that my time is spent both listening and talking, and that the voice I listen to is really His.

There's nothing wrong with talking, unless that makes up 100 percent of your "communication." And remember: God sometimes speaks through other Christians to you. They can be a great source of knowledge. But above all, you need to set everything and everyone aside and ask to hear from God Himself.

Think about this the next time you spend time with God. Can you keep quiet for a while? Even when I'm quiet, my mind strings together thoughts and words, and I end up talking in my head. I am ashamed to say that I boss God around a lot. I whine, and I ask for things, and I make suggestions, and I fill Him in on current events. But I don't stop and listen to what He has to say to me. I'm too used to talking and thinking everything to death. How very embarrassing!

Today . . . this day . . . I will listen. I will remember who He is, and I will listen to *Him*. I wonder what I will hear?

Today I will be still. I will listen and watch, taste, touch, and smell, expecting the One who gave me five senses to speak through them.

"Be still before the Lord and wait patiently for him." (Psalm 37:7—the "don't worry" psalm)

"'Be still, and know that I am God.'" (Psalm 46:10)

## What Else Is There?

Today I'm thinking about that mysterious verse at the end of John's gospel: "Jesus did many other things as well. If every one of them were written down, I suppose that even the whole world would not have room for the books that would be written" (John 21:25).

Ever wonder about what didn't get written down?

Ever wonder why we have so little from those thirty-three years? (Comparatively.)

Ever wonder why we have what we do have?

God has given us a great gift: history recorded through godly authors who knew Him and were inspired to write by God's own Spirit. When you read the New Testament, does it cross your mind that you are hearing the memories and the inspirations of people who actually knew Jesus in the flesh . . . talked to Him . . . would recognize His voice on the phone? (Yeah, I know . . . no phones.) When you remember that, it's pretty impossible not to read with exclamation points and excitement. God not only gave these authors His Spirit to help them write, but He also gives us the same Spirit to help us read and understand.

John knew Jesus very well. I think of him trying to explain this God/man, his best friend, to a world that needed to understand, and I am amazed that he could leave anything out. The Spirit directed John to record enough for us to know salvation and to pursue "life to the full" (John 10:10). But there just is no way any book can contain the hugeness of God, or all the thoughts and works of Jesus. Some wonderful things must have been left unrecorded.

Sometimes I wonder about all the days in between the New Testament stories. What miracles don't I know about? What stories have I never heard? I wonder how Jesus would have reacted to some of the situations I have faced.

The more I wonder, the more desperately I want to know Him, not just the stories about Him. That will take a lifetime . . . and an eternity!

Do some wondering today. Think BIG.

> "Jesus did many other things as well. If every one of them were written down, I suppose that even the whole world would not have room for the books that would be written." (John 21:25)

## Just Like the Moon

John Piper, in his book about missions, *Let the Nations Be Glad*, identifies one basic principle about serving God, which is both simple and significant: God created us to praise Him, to be glad and to rejoice, and if we would just give our lives to this, we would see Him accomplish what He intended when He created us.

> God is most glorified in you when you are most satisfied in him! The great sin of the world is not that the human race has failed to work for God so as to increase his glory, but that we have failed to delight in God so as to reflect his glory.

What a great reason to exist—to be satisfied in God!

Think of your personality as an instrument, specially created to reflect God's glory. Does this mean you need to do something that makes Him look good? Does it mean your life must be spent keeping rules and performing religious functions? No, no! That's not it at all! You and I are called just to shine with reflected light. Just as the moon reflects light from the sun, so we reflect the light of God's glory. Without the sun, the moon is just a dark mass in space. Neither can we generate any light on our own. It's all about *His* glory.

God knows exactly where you are and has given you the opportunity to be what He created you to be in your particular situation. God isn't random. He knows what He's doing, and He asks of us what is possible. Your mission is to be satisfied in God and reflect His glory!

What will that look like today?

> "The Lord reigns, let the earth be glad; let the distant shores rejoice." . . . "May the peoples praise you, O God; may all the peoples praise you. May the nations be glad and sing for joy, for you rule the peoples justly and guide the nations of the earth." (Psalm 97:1; 67:3–4; see also Psalms 16:11; 37:4; 69:32; 70:4)

## Science

My dad taught science, and he was good at it. He had this wonderful ability to look at the world and see how things worked and fit together. He spent many hours patiently teaching me to see little things, to hear quiet things, and to think big things.

Dad used the intelligence God gave him to run down all possibilities when he was seeking an answer. Belief in God did not limit his scientific mind, nor did it offend his intellectual capabilities. Dad believed that God was bigger than any human mind could comprehend, and that people are born with a God-given desire and the ability to ask questions and seek truth. For him, science provided a look into some of the mysteries of the Creator.

C. S. Lewis, in *Miracles*, had this to say about God and science:

> In science we have been reading only the notes to a poem;
> in Christianity we find the poem itself.

So often we limit ourselves to the notes of the poem. We listen only to explanations given by finite people about the world and about right and wrong. But the notes mean nothing if we aren't familiar with the poem.

God's story is simple. The plot and the details are complex. Today, look for the big, simple story, not the tedious details. Life and freedom are in that simple story. That is not to say the details are unimportant. But make sure you keep the main thing the main thing.

God's truth is only underscored by the details science discovers.

"In the beginning God created the heavens and the earth." (Genesis 1:1–2:2)

## Trust Me . . . Really (Part 1)

Have you ever seen a young parent (usually a father) holding a baby up in his arms and then sort of throwing him up in the air and catching him? I don't know what it is about new fathers and uncles that makes them go through this nasty little ritual, but if you ask them what in the world they are doing they will most likely tell you they are teaching the baby about trust. Really! But you look into that cute little chubby face that is used to being cradled and held, being tossed about, and you see eyes that are stretched a bit too wide in absolute terror . . . and you wonder: Is this how a child learns trust?

With my own kids, the terror only lasted for a little while. Then they figured out, "Okay. This guy catches me. Then he laughs and holds me close. Maybe this is fun." From then on when their daddy would launch them into the air over his head they would begin to squeal and giggle. They were learning trust, but it wasn't a universal trust. They were learning specifically to trust Daddy because he always caught them.

The trust lessons continued as the kids were dared to jump off the side of the bed into Dad's waiting arms at the count of 3 . . . to jump off a diving board to a water-treading Dad gurgling, "I've got you!" My kids have learned what to expect from a consistent dad, and they have learned to trust him.

But what if they hadn't been cautioned about whom to trust? What if they were simply conditioned to jump when any voice counted to three? What if they were never taught to think through consequences as a part of knowing what and whom to trust? I remember watching helplessly from across the room as my son tottered on the edge of the couch, yelled "two, free!" and plummeted to the unforgiving floor. He learned the hard way that trust needs to be earned and learned, and that faith needs to be *in* somebody or something.

Spend some time in prayer today asking God to remind you of times He has caught you. Maybe it was at the death of a loved one, when you felt a peace that made no sense to you. Maybe it was a close call on the highway. Thank Him for being there and teaching you to trust in Him.

He will always catch you.

"The eternal God is your refuge, and underneath are the everlasting arms." (Deuteronomy 33:27)

## Trust Me . . . Really (Part 2)

"Just think of the tragedy of teaching children not to doubt."

—Clarence Darrow

When I read this quote the first time, I didn't know what to think of it. But the more I've mulled it over, the more I believe there is something to it.

I don't know of many Sunday schools that teach kids how to doubt. We sing "Trust and Obey" and we hope kids will learn to walk by faith. But do we spend enough time teaching them to think—to discern whom and what to trust?

When a child does not learn critical thinking skills, her faith becomes more wishful thinking than rock-solid fact. What good does it do for a child to trust in God to make her pass a test for which she hasn't studied? Or to protect him even though his behavior is foolish and reckless? Where do we learn the parameters of trust? Where do we learn to ask the right questions and to doubt the easy answers? Not everyone who speaks of God is trustworthy. Not all of the promises we claim and the verses we quote mean what we may have twisted them to say. Before something can be trustworthy it has to be true!

Have you learned to ask hard questions in matters of your faith? Questions like: "Where is that written? Who said that? Who was that promise given to? Does it even apply to me?" These are questions that will confirm and build up your faith.

What do you do when you have doubts? Have you struggled with the things you've been told about God until you have come to believe out of your own experience, not just out of mindless acceptance? What if someone goes beyond asking what you believe to ask you why you believe it? God would much rather have you try Him out and seek evidence of His trustworthiness than to have you just go through the motions of religion. God is not surprised or threatened by the doubts of an earnest seeker!

Facing your doubts in the presence of God is how real faith and trust develop. Making sure you understand what you believe, and that it fits with the character of God, requires an ability to discern His voice in the things you read, hear, and learn. You really need to know how to recognize His voice. Otherwise you may find yourself jumping when just anybody counts to three.

Faith, after all, is not the same as gullibility!

> "'My sheep listen to my voice; I know them, and they follow me. I give them eternal life, and they shall never perish; no one can snatch them out of my hand.'" (John 10:27–28)

## Help Yourself!

I'm sitting in a little stream of sunshine that is pouring through my window. What a great way to start a day.

In my devo for this morning I read that the apostle Paul lived in such a way that "wherever he went, Jesus Christ helped Himself to his life" (Oswald Chambers). Is that an amazing thought or what?

Even the idea that Jesus would *want* to help Himself to somebody's life is a challenge—but wherever He went?

That's a good question for this day. What about my life in this very minute would Jesus want to claim as His own? If I let Him help Himself to my life, what would He do with it . . . right now, right here, in this day and in this place? Suppose I gave total control of my mind, my heart, my schedule to Jesus. What would change in the way this day unfolds?

Think I'll go ponder that one over a cup of coffee. (Hmm. I wonder if Jesus likes coffee.)

> "And whatever you do, whether in word or deed, do it all in the name of the Lord Jesus, giving thanks to God the Father through him." (Colossians 3:17)

## Slimy Pits and Mud

> "I waited patiently for the Lord; he turned to me and heard my cry. He lifted me out of the slimy pit, out of the mud and mire; he set my feet on a rock and gave me a firm place to stand. He put a new song in my mouth, a hymn of praise to our God." (Psalm 40:1–3)

There isn't one of us that won't get hit with the bad side of life one time or another. I've been through my share of stuff, just as you have. But today I want to turn around to you, look you in the eye, and give you encouragement and hope. Keep on! It gets better . . . really. Just keep on.

Sometimes we stay in the "slimy pit of mud and mire" for what seems like a long time. But the key to getting out is simple. Don't

138

fight the mud. Don't waste energy swearing at the slimy pit. Just go to God, cry in His arms, and wait. One day you'll notice something firm under your feet—something that begins to feel like safety and confidence once more. So just hold on until God plants your feet again.

Broken hearts get better. Lost relationships can turn from bitter sadness to sweet memories. Disappointments can be forgotten! We just can't do it ourselves. Only God can take the poison out of tragedy. Only He can help us escape from the mud and mire. He will not be defeated by sadness, evil, or death. If we give our heartaches and depression to Him, He will handle them in His time—and then surprise us with a "new song in our mouths . . . a hymn of praise to our God."

This is no "positive thinking" stuff. This is the clearly marked EXIT from a time of bitterness and brokenness, confusion, or despair.

My prayer for you today is that you have a song of praise in your mouth. If you do, watch for those who are still waiting and pray with them . . . encourage them. If you don't, just hold on. The only time sorrow or trouble can defeat you is if you insist on handling it yourself. Give it to the One who has never lost a battle. Ever.

"We wait in hope for the Lord; he is our help and our shield. In him our hearts rejoice, for we trust in his holy name. May your unfailing love rest upon us, O Lord, even as we put our hope in you." (Psalm 33:20–22)

# Heaven

I had a great conversation with an old friend this past week and she told me that she thinks heaven sounds a bit boring if all it is is praising God . . . non-stop. I've been thinking about that, and I've decided that my friend is wrong.

When a person does what God has made her to do, and does it the best she can, I think that is praise. My life is praise to God when He is my focus and I do what He has gifted me to do. Well, wouldn't living in eternal praise be that we are each doing what we do, and doing it well? I mean, some folks sing—that's their thing—but is that the definition of praise for everyone? How about an athlete pushing personal limits to reach excellence? If that is done with God as the focus, wouldn't that be praise? How about an artist expressing images of beauty as God reveals them? How about relaxing and totally enjoying God's creation? That brings me to praise every time.

So, I'm thinking "eternal praise" means living in relationship with God as He intended, realizing who He is and who I was created to be, and being able to be that every moment because sin won't keep me from it.

Heaven, I'm afraid, has been given a rather limited and boring definition by the world, when in actuality I think it will be the "life to the full" that Jesus talked about in John 10:10. Not some cloudy, netherworld existence, but real, exciting, and limitless life with God. I believe it will be filled with adventure and discovery, with art and sport and music and dance, with leisure and learning—all unpolluted and unspoiled.

Praise comes from realizing who God is and doing whatever we do to appreciate and love who He is.

Read Psalm 150.

"Let everything that has breath praise the Lord." (Psalm 150:6)

## Fly Well

Intercession is an amazing occupation! As I pray for those God has given me to love, it is a precious conversation with a God who *loves* to hear the names of His children. Today I want only to remind you that your life matters to God.

I can imagine the love in His heart at the mention of your name. Isn't it sweet to think of bringing a smile to someone's face, especially if that someone is God? Deuteronomy 32:10–11 says:

"He shielded him and cared for him; he guarded him as the apple of his eye, like an eagle that stirs up its nest and hovers over its young, that spreads its wings to catch them and carries them on its pinions."

This is what God sees in you: Something precious that He will protect and care for. As a young eagle learns to fly, the adult will fly beneath, giving it a ride, and then standing ready to catch it when it ventures forth on its pinions . . . its feathers . . . its wings. You are the most precious thing in the world to God, and He will catch you, hold you, and teach you to fly.

"For you have been my refuge, a strong tower against the foe. I long to dwell in your tent forever and take refuge in the shelter of your wings." (Psalm 61:3–4)

## Passing Through

Today I received news about death touching a family that I love. And suddenly I am remembering others I have loved who aren't here anymore and I'm thinking about an old gospel song my dad taught me:

This world is not my home, I'm just a passing through.
My treasures are laid up somewhere beyond the blue;
The angels beckon me from heaven's open door,
And I can't feel at home in this world anymore.

(Stamps-Baxter Music)

The Bible tells us that we have an inheritance, kept in heaven, which can never perish, spoil, or fade. It says that we are children of God and strangers to this world, and today that all makes wonderful sense to me. This world just isn't home. It isn't the perfection that God intended. It is a fallen place where people get hurt, and where death separates us from those we love. But somewhere down deep inside we have a longing—a hope—for something perfect. Do you know what I mean?

I want to know what total faithfulness and trust are like, and joy that will not ever diminish. I don't want to fail anymore or see people I love cry. I want a safe place where things will be as they should be, and where things will make sense. Somewhere deep down I know those things are right . . . and possible.

C. S. Lewis wrote, "If I find in myself a desire which no experience in this world can satisfy, the most probable explanation is that I was made for another world."

This world is just preparation for another very real world. Thank God He loved us so much that He would come to a place like this with a personal invitation to life as He means it to be. Live today in the hope of that other, very real world.

> "Praise be to the God and Father of our Lord Jesus Christ! In his great mercy he has given us new birth into a living hope through the resurrection of Jesus Christ from the dead, and into an inheritance that can never perish, spoil or fade—kept in heaven for you." (1 Peter 1:3–4)

## This Day

As I finished praying for you guys today I filled up with such a wonderful feeling of anticipation! This is a new day . . . no one has ever seen it before. In it are hidden the secrets of heaven itself. God is preparing us, with everything that enters our lives this day, to know Him more intimately. Watch for Him. Expect to hear Him.

When the beautiful delights you, seek Him in it. When the difficult challenges you, find Him there. When disgusting and unholy things affront you, seek refuge in Him. When failures and sins snatch up bits of your energy, give them into His hands. When victory and triumph make you feel wonderful, let Him have that too.

Anything you face today is something you can share with God, and in doing that, your day will most definitely NOT be ordinary. Don't settle for anything less than a day spent in the presence and power of God. Each event of this day has the potential of making you more like Him. Amazing!

Notice everything. Waste nothing.

"If anyone is in Christ he is a new creation; the old has gone, the new has come!" (2 Corinthians 5:17)

## The Main Thing

"Who am I?" "Where am I going?" "What's my purpose in life?" These are the questions that each of us, at one time or another, ask ourselves. And we can't find the answer by comparing ourselves to anyone else. At the end of the day, each of us stands alone before God and our true identity is revealed—not discussed, proved, or argued. Whether I have accomplished great things or small things, whether I am loved or hated, whether people know me or have never heard my name is not relevant. All that will count on that day is what I did when I heard the call of God.

And make no mistake . . . He calls to each of us every single day of our lives.

We're used to thinking in terms like "great" and "ordinary." But those are labels of pride that are plastered on life by people with a very limited perspective. In God's eyes those labels are ridiculous. He asks only that we obey, not that we evaluate our assignments and obey according to their worth. In His terms, the only successful life is one lived in response and obedience to His call.

When Jesus called His disciples and they responded, they didn't follow Him because of their faith or ability. It was an act of obedience. They didn't know enough to understand why they obeyed, but something in hearing that voice let them know it was the voice of authority for them. So they followed—one day, one moment, at a time.

God's "call" on our lives is far more than a one-time revelation of direction. It isn't just a call to an occupation or a position; it is His voice specifically to you and me, pointing out what should occupy the very next moment.

It is much, much easier to follow Jesus into positions of leadership and recognition than it is to follow Him through the hours of this day. I believe that one day, when we gain God's perspective on "great" and "ordinary," we will find that persevering with excellence in the ordinary things was the main thing He wanted from us.

Keep the main thing the main thing.

> "And whatever you do, whether in word or deed, do it all in the name of the Lord Jesus, giving thanks to God the Father through him." (Colossians 3:17)

## How's Your Mug?

I picked up a cup of coffee in the kitchen this morning and popped it in the microwave to reheat. Then I took several gulps and as I got to the bottom of the mug—well, let's just say it wasn't very pretty. It wasn't the mug I started out with this morning! So I got a clean mug and started over with fresh coffee. And all I can say is that it is definitely nicer to get to the bottom and find, well, nothing. Something to be said for a clean cup.

I'm thinking that's what God wants to happen with us, especially if we are trying to pour ourselves out into the lives of others. Every so often He needs to scrub us . . . get the crud out . . . so that people will get the blessing of what we have to offer without the nasty shock of realizing we're serving out of a dirty cup.

The apostle Paul said that he was being poured out like a drink offering, and I'm thinking, the reason Paul's offering was so powerful was that when he was poured out, there was no crud in the bottom of the cup. He was able to offer folks the Living Water of Christ without polluting it, and without disgusting them with a soiled testimony.

Ever have an encounter with a well-meaning Christian that leaves you feeling offended, and you can't really put your finger on why? What they say is true, but somehow the Living Water just doesn't taste right. I'm thinking that's why Jesus says to go and get things right with our brothers before we take communion—to keep things clean and tasting right.

Hmmm . . . forgiveness for the sake of keeping the taste of Christ unpolluted. Interesting thought. Keeping my heart clean for Christ's sake!

Today I feel clean, at least for this moment, and it's good. I'm so glad we have unlimited do-overs on forgiveness!

Roll around in the sweet, sweet gift of forgiveness as you celebrate the One who bought it for us.

Read Psalm 51.

"Cleanse me with hyssop, and I will be clean; wash me, and I will be whiter than snow." (Psalm 51:7)

## You Still Here?

This morning I keep remembering a quote from an excellent book, *Grasping God's Word* by J. Scott Duvall and J. Daniel Hays:

> The student sitting next to Albert Einstein turned to
>     him and asked, "What do you do?"
> Einstein replied, "I am a student of physics. What do
>     you do?"
> "Oh," the student answered, "I finished studying
>     physics last year."

Here is my prayer for you this week: May you go to the Word with fresh eyes, expecting that your study will yield new and effective ways to connect ancient truths with modern ears and hearts. The stories you know the best might be the very ones in which hidden pearls of the kingdom still lie uncovered. I ask the Lord to give you a joyful passion in your studies, and that you never be fooled by the enemy when he whispers to you that you already know enough.

Brothers and sisters, we've only begun. May the things you prepare to share with others do their work on you first.

The way I figure it, if I wake up in the morning and I'm still here . . . there's something new for me to learn. Hey, you woke up this morning still here, right?

> "Oh, the depth of the riches of the wisdom and knowledge
> of God!" (Romans 11:33)

## Playing in the Sand

I'm thinking this morning about God's people . . . the ones He led out of Egypt with Moses all those years ago. You know the story. The ten plagues hit Pharaoh and the Egyptians, and the Israelite people walk away with riches and cattle. As the amazing story continues, God's people escape through a parted sea, get water from a rock, and get their roadmap from a pillar of fire at night and a cloud by day.

What's hard to understand, at least in hindsight, is what happened when they finally got ready to cross into the Promised Land. The majority voted no! Only two guys were ready to go. Unbelievable, after all God had done for them and with them. But God honored their choice—and they stayed in the desert for forty years!

Forty years of wandering around is a long time. If you check out Deuteronomy 1:2 you'll find a little parentheses that says, "(It takes eleven days to go from Horeb to Kadesh Barnea by the Mount Seir road.)" Forty years for an eleven-day journey! God was ready for His people to move on, but they opted to wander around and play in the sand.

Here's my thought. The Christian life is supposed to be abundant, but there may be some things in our behavior that we need to change before we can enjoy that abundance. Abundant life is our promised land. What things could we fix in eleven days that we have been living with for years? Temper? A habit that we think is unimportant, even though we know it isn't good? Our knowledge of Christ? The promised land—the abundant life—is right there. Are we still playing in the sand?

It's time to deal with whatever is keeping you in the desert. Make time today for God to point that thing out to you and get ready to move on.

> "The Lord our God said to us at Horeb, 'You have stayed long enough at this mountain. . . . See, I have given you this land. Go in and take possession. . . .'" (Deuteronomy 1:6, 8)

## Being Ready

Whatever else people may say about the apostle Paul, one thing that must be said is that he took every opportunity to share what was important in his life. When Paul was on trial before Governor Festus and King Agrippa, they said, "So, Paul, tell us about yourself" (paraphrase of Acts 26:1). So he stood up boldly and talked about God the way some folks talk about themselves. Paul had been so invaded by the Spirit of God that he couldn't talk about himself apart from God.

When Paul was finished, the king said, "You are so convincing that you may soon convert me!" (Acts 26:28 as understood by many commentaries).

How many times in the next week will we face opportunities where somebody says, "So, tell me about yourself"? It probably won't be a king who asks, but it might be a boss or a teacher, a doctor or a politician, a student or a parent, a friend. And at that moment we have the same open door that Paul had. I wonder . . . is the story of *you* so full of the Spirit of God that talking about yourself gives Him the spotlight? Amazing thought. So often we think of evangelism or giving our testimony as a religious thing we set out to do, when in fact it should be done just in how we talk about ourselves.

Peter says in 1 Peter 3:15, "Always be prepared to give an answer to everyone who asks you to give the reason for the hope that you have." Can't you just see Peter practicing that? Can't you see Paul walking along, rehearsing God's goodness to him? I can.

Be ready. You never know who may ask, and who may end up saying to you, "I am almost convinced because of what you say!"

> "But in your hearts set apart Christ as Lord. Always be prepared to give an answer to everyone who asks you to give the reason for the hope that you have. But do this with gentleness and respect, keeping a clear conscience, so that those who speak maliciously against your good behavior in Christ may be ashamed of their slander." (1 Peter 3:15–16)

## Extraordinary Things

I'm sitting at the kitchen table with books spread out, trying to make deadlines and finish projects, and I'm thinking that I don't want my work to be ordinary. Have you ever just gotten tired of the same old same old, and you long for something extraordinary? I think I'll try to make that my new prayer goal—asking God for the extraordinary. The problem is that I've asked that before, and here I sit with the same old ordinary thoughts. God, I want it now! I want to make a difference and be excellent . . . beyond excellent! I wait, and I grow impatient. What's wrong with right now? I'm ready.

Jake and Maggie, our dogs, are driving me nuts today. I'm trying to ignore them, but they keep going to the door and whining. So I let them out and they're right back at the door whining to get in. I know what they want. They want a walk. If they'd just be still for a while I could finish what I'm doing and then I'd be ready to go on a walk with them. They don't understand that I'm the human around here. We go when I'm ready. Whiney time is wasted time.

Once again the dogs grin secretly, knowing they have taught me yet another lesson about God and life. I have a tendency to get a bit whiney in my prayers. "God, I want this, and God I want that . . . teach me this, no that . . . no give me rest . . . or maybe an adventure." Asking God for extraordinary things is a right thing to do, but until He's ready to walk me into those extraordinary adventures I need to be patient and to prepare, in the expectation that *in His time*, we will head out on our walk. And waiting is hard because deep down somewhere, when I forget who He is, I think God is letting opportunities pass by.

Ask for the extraordinary, then sit and be still, expectantly, in His presence. Extraordinary experiences with God nearly always mean that further preparation is required. So I'll keep asking and waiting and preparing. Doesn't seem to be much good in whining. I'll go when He's ready.

> "'Call to me and I will answer you and tell you great and unsearchable things you do not know.'" (Jeremiah 33:3)

> "We wait in hope for the Lord; he is our help and our shield. In him our hearts rejoice, for we trust in his holy name." (Psalm 33:20–21)

# A New Name for God

A young friend spent this weekend with me. She is a wonderful, intelligent young woman who has a burning desire to know God better, and as we talked of Jesus, the conversation turned to "random" things that were happening in her life. She wasn't being hit by lightning bolts as she read or prayed, but she was noticing an increase in the "random" occurrences of her life. As we talked of people who had meant a lot to her in years past, one of those very people showed up at my door. "That was random!" she laughed.

She went to church with us on Sunday morning, and we sang a song she had never heard before. "Funny," I whispered, "that song was played at E and K's wedding"—the sweet person who had "randomly" showed up at my house the day before. The song was about the holy presence of God living in us. I looked my young friend right in the eye and said, "You know, *random* is just another name for the Holy Spirit."

Isn't coincidence funny? Something is on our mind and it just shows up in our day. We think of a friend we haven't thought of in years, and we hear from him or her in a letter or a phone call. We call this coincidence—or as my friend says, "random"—when Scripture tells us plainly that the Holy Spirit Himself will guide us and remind us of the things we need to know. Some days, I dare say, we have actual encounters with God where we don't even recognize Him. We don't even recognize the Spirit that lives within, or the familiar voice or prompting of Jesus!

Random? Coincidence? Think again before you use those words irreverently. They may just be another name for God.

"'All this I have spoken while still with you. But the Counselor, the Holy Spirit, whom the Father will send in my name, will teach you all things and will remind you of everything I have said to you. Peace I leave with you; my peace I give you. I do not give to you as the world gives. Do not let your hearts be troubled and do not be afraid.'" (John 14: 25–27)

## A Royal Pain, My Pleasure

Does just talking about what you have to do this week or this month stress you out? Are you are so busy that you need to grab whatever free minutes you can find just to worry about the next thing on your list?

I know there are times when you have papers due or tests to study for or deadlines to meet or jobs to be done or plans to make or responsibilities to carry out. But for the sake of the machinery that runs you, take a little time to be alone and to pray. I'm not saying this has to be extended quiet time, nor am I suggesting journaling, reading, group stuff—all good things to do, but not primary. First and foremost, you need to spend a few minutes just sitting in the Father's lap and listening to His heartbeat. You need to find the time . . . no, you need to *make* time to do it.

In Mark 1:21 and following we find Jesus in the midst of a very busy day. He has been healing and teaching and casting out demons. He is becoming extremely popular, and everybody wants something from Him. (You think your schedule is tough!) So Jesus decides He needs time to be with the Father, and He finds it. "Very early in the morning, while it was still dark, Jesus got up, left the house and went off to a solitary place, where he prayed" (Mark 1:35).

I don't know about you, but I don't have healing and miracles on my list of things to do today. So what reason could there possibly be for me not to call a timeout for a few minutes just to be with God?

What are you doing for the next five minutes that can't wait?

> "'When you pray, go into your room, close the door and pray to your Father, who is unseen. Then your Father, who sees what is done in secret, will reward you.'"
> (Matthew 6:6)

## When the Clock Strikes Tuesday

My dog can count to eight. Honest.

All night long the clock keeps time, chiming every fifteen minutes and dinging off the hours on the hour. Jake doesn't budge at 5:00 or 7:00 A.M. But as soon as he hears eight, his tail starts thumping on the floor and he begins making a little whiney noise. If it gets to 8:03 and I still haven't paid attention, he comes over and gives me a nudge. If I still don't respond, he goes into the laundry room and sits next to his bowl, letting out a large sigh every few minutes. Jake is serious about breakfast.

He does the same thing at 5:00 P.M. As the clock strikes, he gets all excited. Sometimes we'll be out on the deck where he can't hear the clock, but he gets the time right anyway. It's amazing.

Anyone can develop a habit. If it's a habit that is good for you, we call it a discipline. Jake is disciplined where food is concerned.

So it's Tuesday, and the habit of loving you guys drives me to a place where I get fed—time spent with God in His Word and in prayer for you. Today I am praying that somehow this habit will become yours too. Wouldn't it be cool if every Tuesday for the rest of your life you will hunger to pray for someone you love? Somebody you know needs you to remember him or her regularly.

Do it. God will meet you there every time.

> "'Blessed are those who hunger and thirst for righteousness, for they will be filled.'" (Matthew 5:6)

## Begin Again

As I sat in my dark living room this morning, watching the flicker of a candle and being filled with desire to sit in silence and listen . . . straining for that word . . . that picture . . . that feeling of the presence of the Spirit of God . . . my mind was filled with a most amazing thought. Jesus said that He came to be an example, so that we could do what He did. He didn't say that He was an example for men to be manly like Him and that women should follow the example of someone else. He came to be my example—not of what to *do*, but of what to *be*. Mine.

The One who decided which chromosomes to give me . . . the One who formed me in my mother's womb and wrote every day of my life in His book before one of them came to be (Psalm 139) . . . the One who gave up total freedom and power to be a helpless, vulnerable baby out of love for me . . . He has called me to follow Him. He has created me to be like Him.

Words fail. Tears come. How? I am *not* like Him. I can't heal illness or change the weather. I can't look at my life without regret or forget when I forgive. Temptations get the better of me and I am selfish.

Somewhere in the ear of my heart I hear agreement. Somewhere deeper than my own grief are Divine tears and a passionate pleading: "This is where we begin. You can't. I can. Begin again."

Begin where? "In the beginning was the Word and the Word was with God and the Word was God." Be like the Word.

What did the Word do when He was flesh? What did He spend His human life learning and teaching? What were all the stories and miracles about? What was first on His list? "Love the Lord your God." Knowing the love of God—the Love that is God—*was* His list. To know Love . . . I mean to really, confidently, personally, and passionately know Love—not the emotion but the person— that is to follow the example of Christ. Nothing else can come first. Until I know, what I do will be guesswork.

After all these years, what is it that makes me fall down? I still don't know as I am known. I still need to squint and try to focus. I still try to earn love. Honestly! Try to earn Love? If I think I can earn it, I really don't know Love at all.

To understand the unimaginable love of God. For me? Until I can take it in with no exceptions or excuses, I have not begun. Nothing else matters.

Begin again today. Take the time and begin again. "In the beginning was the Word." Every time.

Read John 1:1–14.

> "The Word became flesh and made his dwelling among us. We have seen his glory, the glory of the One and Only, who came from the Father, full of grace and truth." (John 1:14)

# Shalom

How many times will I read this book, the Bible, and still my mind isn't sharp enough, or large enough to take it all in? Sometimes I feel so limited, so dull. But here is comfort for that. Oswald Chambers said, "Our capacity in spiritual things is measured by the promises of God." In other words, it really doesn't matter how educated we are or what natural abilities we have, nor does it matter how we feel on any given day. What matters is what God has promised.

So, here's a promise for today (Jesus is speaking here):

> "'Peace I leave with you; my peace I give to you. I do not give to you as the world gives. Do not let your hearts be troubled and do not be afraid.'" (John 14:27)

How many times have you read the stories of Jesus? Do you remember the one where He threw down the scrolls in the temple, shouted "I just can't take this anymore!" and ran off to hide in the desert for a while? No? You're right. You never heard it because it never happened. Know why? Because Jesus had shalom (inner peace, joy, and the fullness of life). The very people He came to save hated Him, and the religious leaders were planning to kill Him, but He never lost His kindness or His confidence and He never ran away. Because of that peace. Shalom.

The promise for you today is that He said "My peace I give to you."

Walk through this day like someone who believes that. Some days you might not feel it, but then peace isn't a feeling. It's a condition of the heart—a positive state of rightness and well-being that comes only from God (*The NIV Study Bible*, note on Numbers 6:26). When the heart is right, no situation can undo your confidence if you remember that you have this resource—the same inner peace and joy that Jesus has. How sad is it that people choose to ignore the fact that they already have God's peace and try to handle things physically or emotionally without ever using that spiritual resource.

You don't need to intellectualize it or understand it. Just accept it as a promise and a fact. Don't act until the peace is in place.

> "'Peace I leave with you; my peace I give you. I do not give to you as the world gives. Do not let your hearts be troubled and do not be afraid.'" (John 14:27)

### Holy

Here's one thing I know. God is holy. (Pure, nothing but perfection. Too much good for us to even begin to comprehend.)

Hold on to that one thing this week. What difference will it make to remember that God is holy? It's a huge thing! It means that when the wheels fall off in your own life, one thing will remain constant for you: GOD IS STILL HOLY. That's something that doesn't change. It's something secure to hold on to. It's like always having a point of reference on your journey to keep you from getting too far off the course or from getting lost altogether. No matter where we wander and no matter what messes we may walk ourselves into, God is still there and he is still holy.

Don't confuse God with your circumstances. Don't think that when things are difficult it's because He has made a mistake.

Satan's favorite weapons against us are despair, isolation, and confusion. The holiness of God is like a handle where we just hang on until things calm down some. I may be struggling and I may be confused, but at least I can hold on to this one thing that connects me with my home. My God will always be there for me, and he will only act toward me in ways that befit a holy God. I can always come home to him. I am always welcome to worship a holy God.

Remember, though the sky above and around you may be dark, stormy, and scary, as you come into the presence of the holy God you'll realize that it's only dark outside.

Read Psalm 99.

"The Lord reigns, let the nations tremble . . . let the earth shake. Great is the Lord in Zion; he is exalted over all the nations. Let them praise your great and awesome name." (Psalm 99:1–3)

(Recommended listening: *Worship Together—The Heart of Worship*, "You Are Still Holy," sung by Rita Springer.)

## Sweet and Complete

I planted flowers and dug in dirt yesterday . . . all day. Magnificent day, actually. The fingerprints of God are all over! It's like He paints our world with delicate watercolor strokes all winter . . . grays and shades of blue and green . . . subtle reds . . . washes and hints of things coming. But when spring comes, somewhere out of the depths of nature He coaxes these outrageous colors! I've got one daisy on the deck that's fluorescent orange with a purple center. And how many shades of green are there anyway? I could go on sensory overload just taking a walk on days like these when God kicks everything up a notch! Kind of like the message of Easter repeated in each blade of grass and each budding blossom. "Look here! I'm alive!"

Psalm 19 talks about how nature (particularly the sky) speaks of God. The point being: How could anyone miss this? It's all over! Then the psalm ends with, of all strange things, an appreciation for the laws of the Lord—that God's laws are more precious than gold . . . perfect, reviving the soul. The point being: NOTICE God in creation and let it drive you to His Word.

The psalm wraps up with the hope of a complete day: "May the words of my mouth and the meditation of my heart be pleasing in your sight, O Lord, my Rock and my Redeemer." Cool.

Let God get your attention with His creation; let it drive you to what He has to say in His Word, and then live it, speak it, back to Him. Complete.

I pray for you, my friends, to have a complete day. Not necessarily busy or productive—that's your call—but definitely complete . . . so that when you lay in bed tonight, sleep comes restfully and sweetly to a heart, mind, body, and soul that have lived a complete day. May every flower you see today remind you of the One who made it just to get your attention.

Worship with all five senses today.

Read Psalm 19.

"The heavens declare the glory of God; the skies proclaim the work of his hands." (Psalm 19:1)

## Interpreted by Love

I found this wonderful hymn today, written by John Greenleaf Whittier back in the early 1900s. I guess people got stressed and busy back then too.

Dear Lord and Father of mankind,
Forgive our foolish ways!
Reclothe us in our rightful mind;
In purer lives Thy service find,
In deeper reverence, praise.

In simple trust like theirs who heard,
Beside the Syrian sea,
The gracious calling of the Lord,
Let us, like them, without a word,
Rise up and follow Thee.

O Sabbath rest by Galilee!
O calm of hills above!
Where Jesus knelt to share with Thee
The silence of eternity,
Interpreted by love! . . .

Drop Thy still dews of quietness,
Till all our strivings cease;
Take from our souls the strain and stress,
And let our ordered lives confess
The beauty of Thy peace.

Breathe through the heats of our desire
Thy coolness and Thy balm;
Let sense be dumb, let flesh retire;
Speak through the earthquake, wind, and fire,
O still, small voice of calm.

This morning I am imagining spending a Sabbath day of rest by a lake, sharing the silence of eternity, interpreted by love. Why isn't stillness a priority? Does my "ordered life" confess the beauty of God's peace? Or am I more interested in looking busy? Our priorities and values are all messed up, aren't they?

Find rest today, not only for your sake, but for the testimony such a life gives to the power of the God who lives within. God is in control and there is nothing worth being stressed out over.

> "'Come to me, all you who are weary and burdened, and I will give you rest. Take my yoke upon you and learn from me, for I am gentle and humble in heart, and you will find rest for your souls. For my yoke is easy and my burden is light.'" (Matthew 11:28–30)

## Dehydration

I spent some time in a gym today, hanging out with kids, loving them by taking an interest in their basketball game. (I pray for them and they know that . . . I love my job!) It was really hot, and the kids started dropping. One boy turned rather gray and had to sit out with an awful headache. One girl's heart began to race so that she was at 145/minute, so I sat with her and tried to keep her still. Another girl got light-headed and fell into the bleachers, gashing her knee.

Then I began asking, "Have you eaten?"

"No," they each replied.

"Have you been drinking lots of water?"

"Not really."

They didn't realize that you can't be in the game if you don't take the nourishment of your body seriously. In this heat, lack of water or food can be deadly!

It's the same with your heart and your walk with God, you know. Trying to be in the game without taking the nourishment of your heart, mind, and soul seriously is just as futile . . . the dehydration is just as severe . . . and it can be deadly.

God has told us to pray and to seek Him. Even on days when you don't feel like it, just do it. You need it to live.

> "Trust in the Lord with all your heart and lean not on your own understanding; in all your ways acknowledge him, and he will make your paths straight. Do not be wise in your own eyes; fear the Lord and shun evil. This will bring health to your body and nourishment to your bones." (Proverbs 3:5–8)

### Think

I have been reading in 1 Peter this morning. Listen to this: "Therefore be clear minded and self-controlled so that you can pray" (4:7).

Wow! Keep your head . . . not so that you can figure things out . . . but so that you can pray. I love the thought of needing a clear mind to pray. So often people just get all wordy and religious. You don't need a clear mind for that. But listening and putting together God's Word in the ways He shows us—that takes some mental ability.

I've been thinking about all the things that have not gone the way we have wanted this last year. The death of loved ones in our family, of the broken hearts and the depression some of you have fought. I think of disappointments I've known. Yet God is reminding each one of us: "Be clear-minded and self-controlled so that you can pray!"

God is still God, and God is still good. He sees what's coming tomorrow, and as much as yesterday or today has hurt, He will not waste the hurt. Tomorrow or the next day or the next year . . . that very pain may be what gives you a glimpse of God like you have never even imagined. Trust me. I've seen Him do it. He will take your most awful hurt and allow you to use it to help someone else . . . and suddenly you see what that precious injury looks like when it is sanctified by God.

Be encouraged. Be strong and stubborn. Satan compounds our injuries by confusing us and muddling our thinking. Refuse to let grief or discouragement dictate who God is building you to be. Don't let pain make you a victim.

Nothing is wasted that is given to God! You are His beloved. Never forget that. Expect that God will take the worst Satan can do to you and make it exactly the thing that will defeat him in the end. Don't be overwhelmed. Pray and think with a clear mind.

> "And we know that in all things God works for the good of those who love him, who have been called according to his purpose." (Romans 8:28)

## Recreational Christianity

I am perplexed with easy Christianity. Not because I think we need to work hard, suffer much, earn salvation . . . not at all; but rather because easy Christianity is a lot like recreational sex. We Christians have no problem condemning the world for being intimate with a partner without the commitment and total-life promises of marriage, and yet look what we allow in our own lives. We totally commit our lives to Jesus . . . except of course when we need to be totally committed to the job or to our friends or to our families . . . even to our churches.

If I'm reading Scripture correctly, being a disciple of Jesus demands total intimacy . . . all the time. Yet how few people are consumed 24/7 with Jesus! We think of that kind of devotion as a sacrifice . . . as something hard. Not true! If a heart is truly, totally, intimately given to Jesus, life becomes something more precious and purposeful than anything we could ever imagine or achieve with a lesser commitment. It becomes worship.

Amy Carmichael wrote, "If I myself dominate myself, if my thoughts revolve around myself, if I am so occupied with myself that I rarely have a 'heart at leisure from itself,' then I know nothing of Calvary love."

I marvel at the patience of a God who tolerates the spiritual adultery I allow in my life. How I long to live even one day totally His.

Maybe some of you feel the same way . . . I dearly hope so. Even the longing of our hearts for God is a call to worship.

"With what shall I come before the Lord and bow down before the exalted God? Shall I come before him with burnt offerings, with calves a year old? Will the Lord be pleased with thousands of rams, with ten thousand rivers of oil? Shall I offer my firstborn for my transgression, the fruit of my body for the sin of my soul? He has showed you, O man, what is good. And what does the Lord require of you? To act justly and to love mercy and to walk humbly with your God." (Micah 6:6–8)

## Because He Wanted To?

My husband is out of town on business this week, so I'm letting the dust accumulate. Haven't made the bed since Monday and haven't cooked a meal since Sunday morning. Sweet! I love my sweat pants, wool socks, piles of books all over the floor, and long, wonderful times of loud music and prayer. The sun is out, the sky is blue, the flowers are blooming in my gardens, and my dogs are insane . . . and I think I'll write a psalm.

This morning I let the dogs out in the front yard, and then sent Jake down the driveway to get the paper for me. (Jake is the retriever. Maggie can't be bothered with the whole fetch and obey thing.) So Jake runs out to the street (smiling all the way) and picks up the newspaper . . . and wham! . . . Maggie comes out of nowhere and hits him with a body slam and they both fall over (I'm quite sure I heard them laughing). So I watched them chase each other around trees and bushes, and every time Jake picked up the newspaper, Maggie would slam him again. The paper moved about five feet on each attempt, and by the time it got all the way to me it was all slimy and nasty. I sat out on the porch in my sweats and wool socks, laughing out loud, and totally enjoying how much my stupid dogs were enjoying God's gift of a new day.

You know, I think prayer is a lot like sitting on the front porch in sweats and wool socks on a beautiful morning and being reminded of the personality and the love of a Creator who would make all of this . . . all of us.

Big thought for the day: *Notice* this day and look for something in it that will take your breath away or make you laugh. Then read Revelation 4:11: "Worthy, Oh Master! Yes, our God! Take the glory! The honor! The power! You created it all; it was created because you wanted it." (from *The Message*).

Bigger thought for the day: How about putting your name in the last sentence. "You created me; I was created because you wanted me."

> "'You are worthy, our Lord and God, to receive glory and honor and power, for you created all things, and by your will they were created and have their being.'" (Revelation 4:11)

## Joy

"Joy is peace dancing and peace is joy resting."
—F. B. Meyer

"Joy is the serious business of heaven."
—C. S. Lewis

Joy is evidence that the Spirit of God is alive within your heart, and reminding you of who you were created to be. I have found these things to be true of joy:

1. It is the first thing Satan will try to take away from someone whose heart longs for God.
2. It can't be stolen . . . only given away.
3. It doesn't depend on happiness.
4. It can't be manufactured or faked.
5. It grows out of confidence in truth.
6. Something about joy just feels right . . . like it is the condition in which we were created to live.

Joy is a personality trait of Jesus that the Spirit of God longs to duplicate in you. My prayer for you is that He will succeed. (If you need direction in your quiet time, do a word search in the Bible for "joy" and see what you find.)

> "'Now is your time of grief, but I will see you again and you will rejoice, and no one will take away your joy. . . . Ask and you will receive, and your joy will be complete.'" (John 16:22, 24)

> "Though you have not seen him, you love him; and even though you do not see him now, you believe in him and are filled with an inexpressible and glorious joy, for you are receiving the goal of your faith, the salvation of your souls." (1 Peter 1:8–9)

## If You Can?

One day Jesus came upon a man who had a sick son. Jesus talked to the father for a while and then the man said, "If you can do anything, take pity on us and help us." (Mark 9:22)

Oh, my! Can you imagine talking to Jesus and then saying, "Well, if you can do anything"? Then it hit me like a ton of bricks. That's how most of us pray! We tell God what's going on and then suggest that *if* He can do anything, He could help us out.

So how did Jesus respond? First, He said, "If you can?" (I would imagine the "if" was a little louder than the rest.) "Everything is possible for him who believes" (Mark 9:23).

The guy responded immediately (I'll bet his cheeks were red!) and said, "I do believe; help me overcome my unbelief" (Mark 9:24). Cool answer! He was honest. And Jesus wasn't mad at him. He didn't walk away in a huff. He healed the guy's son. I bet that helped his unbelief!

Here's the point. Doubt isn't a sin. We do two really stupid things. First, we treat God like a mechanic who *may* be able to change our tire. We insult Him with the way we ask for things. Second, we figure that if we don't believe hard enough, God can't do anything.

This day, be honest with God! Tell Him what you need and then ask Him to do what God Almighty can do in a situation. If unbelief is an issue with you, tell Him. (Like He doesn't know already!)

Give your doubt to God and then look for His help in overcoming your unbelief.

If God is God, shouldn't we expect some pretty remarkable things?

Read Mark 9:14–29.

> "'So I say to you: Ask and it will be given to you; seek and you will find; knock and the door will be opened to you. For everyone who asks receives; he who seeks finds; and to him who knocks, the door will be opened.'" (Luke 11:9–10)

# Fear of the Predator

Jon and I were having breakfast out on the deck yesterday morning, and it was really lovely. The birds and squirrels and bugs are so noisy on summer mornings . . . at least they were until a hawk started circling the yard. Bugs aren't interesting to hawks I guess, or maybe bugs are just dumb, because they kept on making buzzing bug noises. But the squirrels and birds all disappeared and became silent . . . an eerie silence. Funny how fear of a predator makes things shut up and hide.

Scripture says a lot about the fact that we have a predator hunting us, too. This enemy "prowls around like a roaring lion looking for someone to devour" (1 Peter 5:8). Satan is doing what comes naturally to a predator . . . he's hunting for you and me. And so often we react the way the hunted naturally do, by hiding in fear and hoping he just goes away. I know I've done that on more than one occasion.

But hiding in fear isn't safety from Satan; it's victory for Satan. Hiding in fear we begin to believe that we are powerless. We forget that we are created in the image of God and that the very Spirit of God lives in our hearts, giving us power to take the offensive. James 4:7 says, "Resist the devil, and he will flee from you." Have you ever seen two or three little birds take off after a larger bird that has invaded their nest? They dive and peck and pester until the big bird flees from them.

Whatever form discouragement or fear takes in your life today—and some days are harder than others, no doubt—don't let it make you run and hide. You are God's priceless possession, and when Jesus redeemed you, He didn't just sort of clean up your nasty human heart. He gave you a new heart, the one He intended for you

. . . in the image of God . . . and then filled it with Himself and all of His power. You have a good heart . . . the heart of a warrior, not a coward.

Whenever Satan attacks you, counterattack immediately with God's truth about who you are. And don't be afraid to call for reinforcements. You never need to fight him alone. Resist him and he will turn tail and run.

Now go live today like someone with a good heart.

Expect something good from yourself today. I do.

> "Be self-controlled and alert. Your enemy the devil prowls around like a roaring lion looking for someone to devour. Resist him, standing firm in the faith, because you know that your brothers throughout the world are undergoing the same kind of sufferings." (1 Peter 5:8–9)

> "Submit yourselves, then, to God. Resist the devil, and he will flee from you." (James 4:7)

## Outrageous

"Jesus loves me, this I know, for the Bible tells me so." I can simply believe in that love. It's a fact. But do I love Jesus? Do you? Is that love an emotion? Does it change with my moods or depend upon my circumstances? Really, take a minute and think. Do you love Jesus?

Oswald Chambers said that we cannot love Jesus on our own. We can admire, respect, and even reverence Him, but passionate love for Christ happens only through the Holy Spirit. "He will take your heart, your nerves, your whole personality, and simply make you blaze and glow with devotion to Jesus Christ."

This is my prayer for you. Not that you will try hard to have devotions, or be good, or work hard in your church. Those are good things, but my prayer is that in addition you will be overtaken with a passionate love for Jesus that seeps out of your eyes, your smile, your voice. Chambers calls that "moral spontaneous originality."

It has been my experience that the more the Holy Spirit controls your heart, the more people will be drawn to engage you in conversation. Being a churchy Christian is not what appeals to folks; in fact, it usually ends conversations with anyone outside of your own church group. But passionate and pure love for Christ is compelling. Especially to a world that doesn't understand such a passion.

"Moral spontaneous originality" delights Jesus. It doesn't always delight religious folks who are working hard to please Christ but have not allowed the Spirit to make them lose control of their lives to Him.  But that's okay. You need to "blaze and glow" wherever God puts you. You need to be a little out of control and totally available to the outrageous control of the Holy Spirit.

That kind of passion just won't stay inside the lines.

Read Acts 6:8–15.

> "Now Stephen, a man full of God's grace and power, did great wonders and miraculous signs among the people. . . . All who were sitting in the Sanhedrin looked intently at Stephen, and they saw that his face was like the face of an angel." (Acts 6:8, 15)

## Come Let Us Adore . . . and Be Adored

*"The Lord bless you and keep you,"*

Today I ask God to supply everything you need for life . . . breath, food, water, shelter.

*"The Lord make His face to shine upon you"*

May you believe in your heart that God looks on you with genuine love.

*"And be gracious to you."*

May you experience the grace that has chosen you, forgiven you, accepted you just as you are.

*"The Lord turn His face toward you"*

Just as a parent takes a child's face in his hands and looks him right in the eyes.

*"And give you peace."*

May you return His gaze and realize that you are safe in his love.

*Shalom*

These are God's words of peace to you. Have you really even begun to imagine that the One about whom we sing, "O come let us adore Him" adores you?

That's a large thought. I don't think we'll ever really "get it." But try.

> "The Lord bless you and keep you; the Lord make his face shine upon you and be gracious to you; the Lord turn his face toward you and give you peace." (Numbers 6:24–26)

## Songs of the Heart

When President Ronald Reagan died in 2004, his funeral was broadcast over all the networks and cable news shows. His favorite hymns were played throughout the ceremonies, and during the times when no one was speaking and nothing formal was happening, you could tune out the babble of the commentators and hear that music in the background.

No one sang the words, but those who know and love those hymns could hear the words—words of truth. "My faith looks up to Thee, Thou lamb of Calvary, Savior divine." . . . "Mine eyes have seen the glory of the coming of the Lord." . . . "Jesus, lover of my soul, let me to Thy bosom fly" . . . "Jesus the very thought of Thee with sweetness fills my breast." Amazing! Fox News, CNN, MSNBC, ABC, NBC, and CBS, all proclaiming Jesus. It was like hearing an encoded message . . . like insider knowledge . . . a secret message . . . all over and behind the political comments. Awesome.

Made me think about what we fill our minds with. When grief or crisis comes and we can't think well for ourselves, the words we hear come from deep down inside our memories . . . the Scripture we know, the songs we love, the truths we have memorized.

I challenge you to think today about the words of songs you listen to. Trust me, they are sticking in your mind. What are you repeating over and over? Is it something that will bring you comfort or strength when you need it? Are they words of truth?

When I am dying and the words from memory are the only thoughts that will come, I'd much rather have my brain fill with, "What a friend we have in Jesus" than with "It's five o'clock somewhere."

Just a thought.

> "I have hidden your word in my heart that I might not sin against you." (Psalm 119:11)

> "How precious to me are your thoughts, O God! How vast is the sum of them! Were I to count them, they would outnumber the grains of sand. When I awake, I am still with you." (Psalm 139:17–18)

## Remember Who's Sleeping in the Front of the Boat

The house I grew up in was a quiet house. There was no background noise, no ignored radio or TV left playing. If words were filling the air, they were intentional. When my mom turned on a favorite radio station or played a favorite record, I noticed . . . and I listened.

I remember one song she especially liked, which spoke of calling out to God when the waves of life were raging, and asking Him to calm the sea. One time when I was very ill, she played that song over and over. It was her way of praying for both of us. She told me later that repeating words of confidence in Jesus helped her find peace. She knew how to come to the Savior she loved and simply say, "Fix this, please."

Sometimes God does ask us to ride little boats into choppy waters. And during those times many of us panic and begin to frantically bail water, trying to keep from sinking. But that's not the way to stay afloat. What we need to do is to focus on the One who never sends us out into a storm alone, and to replace our fear with a great sense of adventure.

Where do we find the ability to ride out our storms in peace? Maybe by repeating words of confidence in Jesus . . . singing songs that remind us of miracles and power. So I'm praying that when we're out on the water today, God will either calm the storm or help us catch an occasional fun wave to ride.

One more thing. Disturbances in your sea have nothing to do with your ability or worth. Funny how quickly some of us claim responsibility for the storms. "If things are difficult in my life, it must be punishment for something I've done."

Listen, my friends. Storms come. And sometimes we just can't fix things.

Here's a picture you might like to keep in your mind: As you face your own personal circumstances that are causing your storm, picture Jesus standing tall beside you, feeling the wind, "Quiet! Be still!" That's a picture that brings a smile to my face.

He'll do that in His own time. In the meantime, remember who is sleeping in the front of the boat.

> "[Jesus] got up, rebuked the wind and said to the waves, 'Quiet! Be still!' Then the wind died down and it was completely calm. He said to his disciples, 'Why are you so afraid? Do you still have no faith?'" (Mark 4:39–40)

(Recommended listening: *Gentle Moments*, "Knowing You Love Me," by Evie Tornquist.)

## Imitation Crabmeat

Have you ever used it? It looks like crabmeat but costs less than half the price. You can put it in salads and sauces, and if you add enough other ingredients, it isn't too bad. After you've eaten it for a while you get used to it, and you might even accept the taste and texture as genuine crabmeat. The truth is, it's whitefish. You can call it crabmeat all day long, but what you're serving up is just a bargain-priced, crabmeat imposter. If I go to a seafood restaurant and order fresh crab, I'd better not get whitefish. If I do, you can bet I won't be going back there. I know the difference because I happen to love the real thing, although I imagine there are people who don't realize the difference because they have never tasted real crab.

Something similar can happen in our faith. If we don't get what's real on a regular basis, it's possible to develop a tolerance for imitations. Programs, studies, events, books—all nice, but none of them are Jesus. They can remind us of Him, but they are not Him. Actual, daily relationship with Jesus is a difficult thing.

Amy Carmichael wrote, "If I forget that the way of the cross leads to the cross and not to a bank of flowers, then I know nothing of Calvary love."

I'm afraid some have invented an easy religion that has people looking for the bank of flowers. Popular American churchianity is trying to reach people by being relevant and presenting a culturally correct, God-endorsed, happy lifestyle which includes no talk of the personal cost of taking up a cross and becoming like Jesus. The sad truth is that hanging out with Christians and doing Christian things just won't save anybody. In our quest not to be offensive to the world, we have kept a lot of the stuff Jesus said, but He's not invited to mess in our lives anymore. I'm thinking, if it's not the real deal, isn't it dishonest to mislabel the product?

Don't offer mediocrity to a starving world. And don't accept it for yourself or your family. Knowing Christianity is not the same as knowing and being known by Jesus. Much in our "Christian" culture should be required to come with a label that reads "no nutritional content."

"Ain't nothing like the real thing, baby!"

> "'Not everyone who says to me, "Lord, Lord," will enter the kingdom of heaven, but only he who does the will of my Father who is in heaven. Many will say to me on that day, "Lord, Lord, did we not prophesy in your name, and in your name drive out demons and perform many miracles?" Then I will tell them plainly, "I never knew you. Away from me, you evildoers!"'" (Matthew 7:21–23)

## Nourishing Prayer

Here's your brain breakfast for today:

> "We hear it said that a man will suffer in his life if he does not pray; I question it. What will suffer is the life of the Son of God in him, which is nourished not by food, but by prayer . . . Prayer is the way the life of God is nourished."
> —Oswald Chambers

Last night Matt, a young friend, came over to the house to hang out for a while. We talked for about three hours, and our conversation was full of Jesus. It wasn't "Christian" talk, but real talk about life and love, funny things, scary things, friends . . . and it was all full of Jesus. And it all happened because of prayer.

Matt has no reason to want to hang out with me other than the bond that has been built between us through the years as I have prayed for him and through the love in Christ that comes from that. Our friendship isn't dependent on age or moods or circumstances . . . only on the love of Jesus that flows between our hearts. This is the life of God in me and in Matt and between Matt and me.

Last week I had several similar conversations with people I am bound to by prayer. What a rich time! So filled with trust and ease and freedom and acceptance. Guess what? This is the body of Christ as it is intended to be. And it can't happen without prayer. Only as we pray for each other does the body of Christ grow and thrive.

Also, when you pray for someone regularly, that prayer affects your own life. You can nourish the life of the Son of God in your own heart right now. It's worth the time to start your day right.

Read Luke 11:1–4.

> "One day Jesus was praying in a certain place. When he finished, one of his disciples said to him, 'Lord, teach us to pray, just as John taught his disciples.'" (Luke 11:1)

## Talking to Strangers

You'll never guess where I am as I pray for you and write this e-mail. I'm sitting in a Laundromat. My purpose? To observe . . . to notice people going about the business of their lives . . . and to ask myself the question, "How would I minister to these folks? How would I begin, and how can I tell them the good news of the gospel in a natural and inoffensive way?"

Know what the common denominator is with most of these people? They don't want to be here! There are some pretty cranky folks going about the business of their lives.

Laundromats are a forced community where people do their best to escape eye contact by watching the TV in the corner or by talking on cell phones. I notice the same thing walking across university campuses . . . a whole bunch of people in close proximity, many of whom are talking with someone who is not there. I even talked to a girl on campus who said that sometimes she just holds her phone to her ear and pretends to be talking so nobody will know how lonely she is. The same is true at airports. Cell phones, newspapers, and TV screens give us a great place to hide and avoid actually talking to the strangers who share our space for a short time. Technology has isolated us into big crowds of lonely people, where we can simply ignore folks who make us uncomfortable.

But if we are trying to become like Christ, can we isolate ourselves this way? I'm thinking of Jesus. He had a close group of good friends and a family He could spend time with. But what made Him so revolutionary were His conversations with strangers. Remember when He was walking through Samaria and struck up a conversation with a woman at a well? Jesus didn't push Himself on her (or anyone). He was friendly and put her at ease so that conversation could happen if she wanted it. And the result? Well, you can ask her yourself one day when you meet her or any of the other inhabitants of her town who are in heaven!

We Christians tend to have an agenda when we encounter strangers. Either we want to get them into a group or we want to save them. Rarely do we just connect for the purpose of showing God's love through friendly concern and conversation.

Funny . . . we think of evangelism as meetings and programs where "they" come to us. Not at all like Jesus, is it?

So today I encourage you to be aware of people . . . especially the cranky ones.

Read John 4:1–42.

> "Many of the Samaritans from that town believed in him because of the woman's testimony, 'He told me everything I ever did.' So when the Samaritans came to him, they urged him to stay with them, and he stayed two days. And because of his words many more became believers." (John 4:39–41)

## Dumb Geese

I can tell summer is ending soon because the geese are practicing their landings and takeoffs on the lake behind the house. Sometimes they come in right over the deck, so close you duck (no pun intended) just out of reflex. There must be a couple hundred of them. They practice hard . . . but they never go anywhere. They never migrate; they stay here all year.

Today these geese bring me a challenge to evaluate the effectiveness of my life as a Christian. I have learned and taught about evangelism with other ministers of the gospel. I have given my testimony to other believers. I have enjoyed fulfilling service within the church and have gone to Christian schools and camps to learn and teach the importance of all that Jesus taught. As good as those things are, however, they are meant to be preparation for a journey . . . *they are not the journey itself.*

This world is *hungry* for the Word of God, but often feeding hungry people who don't know Jesus becomes of secondary importance to our own enjoyment of fellowship with other believers. We have come to know all about Jesus. We may even practice telling each other about Him in the safety of our churches. But we tend to forget that His command to "go into all the world" involves a journey that leads us outside the church and into the world.

Is church the only Christian thing we do? Are we ministering only to each other? Giving testimonies only to ourselves? Just like the dumb geese, are we practicing hard but going nowhere?

The writer of 1 Peter instructs us to "set apart Christ as Lord" in our hearts, and to "always be prepared to give an answer to everyone who asks you to give the reason for the hope that you have"(1 Peter 3:15). Apparently the apostle Peter just assumes that if we *live* Christ, folks will notice and ask about why we live that way. And when they do, we should be ready to give an answer for the hope we have, and do it with gentleness and respect.

Think about that for a minute. People aren't going to ask us why we are different if we are only doing church things. They aren't going to ask if we don't hang out with anyone but Christians. The world has the whole *us vs. them* separation figured out pretty well. We might identify ourselves with a religion (fish on the car, Scripture on the T-shirt), but do we let Christ *take us* to the hungry folks around us?

Jesus drew a ton of attention by hanging out with the hungry people, bringing the peace and hope of God into *their* places. If you do that, folks will ask. (It's like walking into a room with a smile on your face. People want to know what you're smiling about) Then you just relax and tell them.

Don't miss a chance to give someone else your real, personal, first-person accounts of hope.

> "But in your hearts set apart Christ as Lord. Always be prepared to give an answer to everyone who asks you to give the reason for the hope that you have. But do this with gentleness and respect." (1 Peter 3:15)

## Open the Refrigerator!

This past week I've been hearing from a number of people who are in a spiritual slump. "I just can't pray," they say. "I just can't get into reading my Bible." These folks have a deep hunger for the close relationship they once had with God, but they seem to have forgotten how to go about the business of being filled, satisfied, and strengthened. They are suffering from malnutrition.

If this is your situation, listen to this word of common sense and encouragement: EAT SOMETHING! If you want to be close to God, you have to make an effort. If your stomach is rumbling and the fridge is full of food, you aren't going to get fed if you just stand there and look at the door. You need to open it. You need to assume the discipline of taking in nourishment every day.

After God freed the Israelites from slavery in Egypt and led them to safety in the wilderness, it was not long before the people began grumbling (read Exodus 16). They were hungry, so He supplied bread from heaven. The only restriction was that they had to gather it fresh every morning; it would not keep overnight. God kept supplying nourishment, but the people had to go and get it every morning. If they didn't, they went hungry.

I think there's a lesson here for us. Don't try to get nourishment from memories of yesterday's food. And don't plan on getting enough once a week to last you until someone feeds you again. God will provide something fresh for you today, but to get it, you must spend time with Him, in His Word and in conversation with Him. "I am the bread of life," Jesus said. "He who comes to me will never go hungry, and he who believes in me will never be thirsty" (John 6:35).

My dear, hungry friends . . . open the refrigerator!

> "'Blessed are those who hunger and thirst for
> righteousness, for they will be filled.'" (Matthew 5:6)

## I Know You!

I was reading in the book of Nahum today—not the most popular of the Old Testament books. It's pretty violent, talking about God's anger. Then right in the middle of a graphic description of what happens when God is upset comes one little verse that sticks out like a nightlight in a dark house at midnight. "The Lord is good, a refuge in times of trouble. He cares for those who trust in him" (Nahum 1:7).

What a beautiful little gold nugget hidden in these words about God's anger. "Don't forget," He says. "I know you, and I know you trust Me. So don't be afraid."

The next time you are feeling small or insignificant in a scary world, or wondering if you dare stand up for Him in some situation, remember: You aren't alone. God knows you. You can trust Him.

184

"He who dwells in the shelter of the Most High will rest in the shadow of the Almighty. I will say of the Lord, 'He is my refuge and my fortress, my God, in whom I trust.'" (Psalm 91:1–2)

## Backward Theology

This week I met with a young woman who is trying to "have a faith walk" (her words) but has been finding only frustration. We have met together about five times now, and finally the reason for her dilemma came to the surface. It isn't a matter of salvation; it's a matter of misunderstanding grace. Together, she and I have hammered out four misunderstandings that have kept her from the joy of her salvation. Turns out she has had her theology a bit backward.

**Backward theology puts the burden on me.**

If I just say I'm sorry, then I can be forgiven.

If I just work hard enough, I will be accepted.

If I just try hard enough, I will be able to please God.

God needs me to do His work, so I have to deny myself.

**Frontward theology frees me to set my burdens down.**

When I realize my sins are already forgiven, I am free to repent—not out of desperation, but out of gratitude and love.

When I realize that God has accepted me just as I am, I am free to pour all of myself into my work and into my leisure.

When I realize that because of Jesus I am pleasing to God, I can stop trying so hard and just be His.

God doesn't need me to do anything. He is God. The only reason to deny myself is because my love for Him makes me forget myself.

When we let somebody besides Jesus, and some source other than His Word, lay burdens on us, then life is all grunting and groaning, falling down, failing, straining at the bit, rushing and huffing and puffing. Not a pleasing way to give our lives to God.

We too often see a holy finger pointing at us in anger, when the message of the gospel is more like two open hands, palms facing up, fingers curling in, beckoning us to come, enjoy!

Today, I encourage you to live frontward, not backward.

> "Therefore, as God's chosen people, holy and dearly loved, clothe yourselves with compassion, kindness, humility, gentleness and patience. Bear with each other and forgive whatever grievances you may have against one another. Forgive as the Lord forgave you. And over all these virtues put on love, which binds them all together in perfect unity." (Colossians 3:12–14)

## Falling's Not So Bad When Somebody Catches You

I saw a skit last Sunday in which the character was packed and ready to take a trip into the "quagmire" (old, old word for a mucky swamp), and his monologue was about how it was too hard to live at the level he thought Christ wanted, so he would settle for the swamp. The line that caught my attention was "It's easier to sink than to fall."

As I pray for you today I am thinking specifically of the temptations that face women of faith. The biggest temptation of all is the temptation to sink, not fly . . . for fear of a fall. Think of the gender-defined roles we are expected to fill. Churches dutifully teach women about submission, sacrifice, and supporting others, but often neglect to emphasize the fact that these are the most humanly difficult roles in existence. The problem is not in teaching these things, but in teaching *only* these things. There are a few verses that specify things *best done* by a woman, but we can't forget that the rest of the text is meant for us as well. Things like the lists of spiritual gifts—all of them—given at God's discretion to men and women of His choosing.

If we accept the idea that women are weaker or somehow less, we let that be our excuse for settling for a life with no challenge, no trying, no thinking, no discovering, no daring to take God at His word, no excellence, no adventure . . . no flying! Hear me, friends. You are God's beloved, created to enjoy His presence and to be something *nobody else* can be. He has made you intelligent, strong, tender, and creative. He has made you counselors and healers, leaders and servants, and His intention is that you live your life to the full. Only Jesus has the right to define you.

Remember that. Remember who you are. You are invited to walk with Jesus, and that's not boring or safe. Never let anyone take from you your right to try . . . to fly . . . even to fall. Falling's not so bad when Somebody catches you.

Don't settle. Don't sink. Leave no gift unopened. When I physically see Jesus, when this life is done, I want a high-five, a smile, and a "well done!" Because I was great? Hardly! Because I tried. With all my heart, with perpetually skinned knees, and full confidence in our Savior.

> Come to the edge
> "We might fall."
> Come to the edge
> "We might fall."
> COME TO THE EDGE!
> And they came.
> And he pushed.
> And they flew.
> —Guillaume Appollinaire

> "There are different kinds of gifts, but the same Spirit. There are different kinds of service, but the same Lord. There are different kinds of working, but the same God works all of them in all men." (1 Corinthians 12:4–6)

## That's None of Your Business

I just learned something that I hope will change me, and I want to share it with you. It's about pride, and I seem to have a giant, ongoing struggle with it. Maybe some of you can relate. Look at the last part of the gospel of John, after Jesus affirmed Peter and then gave him his marching orders (John 21:15–19). Peter knew he had a hard road ahead, and he had every intention of obeying Jesus because of his love for Him. But then Peter says something I have heard myself (and others) say over and over again. Yeah, but "what about him?" (21:21).

I love Peter because he says the things we all think. Peter thought of his life in comparison to John. I am so guilty of that . . .

comparing my walk to someone else's . . . taking my sense of worth from others. The point is, *others* don't know what Jesus has in store for *me*, or what He has gifted me to do, or what ministry He has set aside only for me. Obedience to Jesus has nothing to do with anything other than hearing Him say "follow Me" and doing just that. But my tendency is to mutter, "Sure, I'm willing to suffer for you, but what about those guys? It's not fair! You're not letting them off the hook, are you?" And Jesus says to me what He said to Peter, "I'll do what I want with them . . . what business is that of yours? You follow Me" (my translation). And I am ashamed to hear myself reply. "Yeah, but it's not fair."

My walk hasn't always taken me in the places I thought it should. Following Jesus has, at times, asked for hard obedience, and although in my heart I want to say, "I'd do anything for you, Jesus!" sometimes I think there really must be a better way than what He says! "I'll be happy to give myself for you . . . but what if nobody notices? What if nobody cares? What if I end up alone? What if I look like a fool? And what about them?" When I allow myself to fall into these selfish questions, the peace of heart that comes from walking with Jesus begins to crumble, and then I hear it . . . I hear Jesus say, "What business is that of yours? You follow Me! Jan! You hard-headed child! Peace will only remain with you as you remember that I will give you your next step. Just you and Me! Trust Me. It's what you need. It's what you really want. It's what I want for you. You need to remember that I will never leave or forsake you!"

And so today I am resolving to live in *my moment*, in *my space*, and stop comparing. God makes no mistakes. Wherever He puts me is the place He wants me to represent Him. That's my business. That's my calling. That is where life to the full is found . . . and peace.

Look today at the exact place God has you. Don't miss where you are because you are thinking about where you are not! *This* is precisely the place where God wants you to reflect Him.

Read John 21:15–25.

"'You must follow me.'" (John 21:22)

## I Can't Bring You Without Bringing Me

I was praying on my knees this morning. It's funny how our posture before the Lord changes our realization of His presence. At least mine does. This morning, as I found myself very low to the floor, the presence of my Intercessor was almost palpable. For one moment it seemed that if I raised my eyes quickly enough I might catch a glimpse . . . just a glimpse. I know there's no way I could see those eyes and ever look away again. But oh . . . just to touch the foot or feel the air stir.

I'll be honest with you. Yesterday was a day of struggle. I encountered someone who always manages to hurt me, and I'm not sure I handled it very well. The heaviness of the encounter felt like one of those lead covers they put on you at the dentist before they x-ray your teeth. But wisdom spoken into the hurt from a very wise young man coupled with a wonderful hour of intercessory prayer this morning has laid the heaviness aside.

Why am I telling you this? Because I want you to know how necessary it is for me to carry you all to God in prayer. I know that seems odd—that when I am in trouble I need to pray for you—but you see, when I bring you into His presence, I also bring myself.

Once again this morning I am in awe of the way God pursues us. He asks me to do something I can do. I can be faithful to pray for you. And I'm not quite sure if this arrangement is because you need it or because I need it. But it brings me where I need to be.

Walk in peace and power, my friends. Pray for each other . . . and maybe you'll be amazed to find yourself in His presence. Trust me, you need it.

> "Let us then approach the throne of grace with confidence, so that we may receive mercy and find grace to help us in our time of need." (Hebrews 4:16)

## God Incognito

> "We may ignore, but we can nowhere evade, the presence of God. The world is crowded with Him. He walks everywhere incognito."
>
> —C. S. Lewis

Today, my world is crowded with God!

My computer does a slide show of all my saved pictures for my screen saver, and as I was trying to concentrate on reading for my next project, up pops a picture of me hugging a dolphin (really). All of a sudden I was transported back to a wonderfully warm day in the Caribbean, standing in waist-deep water as a trained dolphin came up and gave me a hug (actually a kiss too). I remember what his pink belly felt like, so soft and yet so massively huge. I remember his hundreds of tiny little teeth and his eyes. Oh man, it was an excellent experience! I remember being totally amazed that this giant animal was so obedient to the trainer and that I felt no fear at all. I remember spending hours that week just sitting on the beach, looking off across the ocean and praising God. I mean, sometimes God just overwhelms you, doesn't He?

Later I took a walk with my dogs and started to notice things. The trees are changing colors. There are bright berries on bushes back in the woods where nobody ever looks, and there are squirrels and birds . . . there are noises and smells, the feel of warm sunshine and cool breezes. How could I miss this stuff! How could I look right past these marvels of creation and not be swept up in amazement? How could magnificent things become invisible to me? If you don't see a hundred things that defy explanation before bed tonight, you are missing the show. And then talk to the Creator. Just tell Him you noticed.

> "By the word of the Lord were the heavens made, their starry host by the breath of his mouth. He gathers the waters of the sea into jars; he puts the deep into storehouses. Let all the earth fear the Lord; let all the people of the world revere him. For he spoke, and it came to be; he commanded, and it stood firm." (Psalm 33:6–9)

## Baseball and Brother Lawrence

I love baseball. One reason I can enjoy baseball is that I know baseball. I know the rules, some history, and lots of personalities. I've watched it and played it, watched my kids play it, and have many wonderful memories of Cubs games and White Sox games while we lived in Chicago. It's easy for me to close my eyes and let myself soak in the experience of sticky feet, getting sunburned and frozen in the same game, the smell of hot dogs and peanuts, and getting caught up in a common frenzied passion as a part of a crowd. Yeah, I love baseball. Getting to know baseball is what has fueled my passion for it.

Which leads me to Brother Lawrence. (I know, my mind works in mysterious ways.) No, he's not a shortstop. He's a monk who lived in the mid-1600s and is known for his desire to practice the presence of God.

"Let all our employment be to know God; the more one knows Him, the more one desires to know Him," said Brother Lawrence. "And as knowledge is commonly the measure of love, the deeper and more extensive our knowledge shall be, the greater will be our love, and if our love of God were great, we should love Him equally in pains and pleasures."

What if we pursued God with the same passion we have for sports or music or our jobs? Memorizing trivia and facts about our favorite hobby or pastime enables us to enjoy and to speak the language. Suppose the "trivia" we spent our time learning was truth about God? Would that enable our conversations and further fuel our passion for Him? Think of the last brand-new thing you learned about God . . . something you never thought of or knew before. Was it today? Yesterday? Recently?

If you learned one new thing about God each week, it would drastically alter your ability to love Him. What could be more worthwhile than getting familiar with the character of God for the express purpose of loving Him better?

"His divine power has given us everything we need for life and godliness through our knowledge of him who called us by his own glory and goodness." (2 Peter 1:3)

193

## That Thing Got a HEMI?

Reading Ephesians 1 this morning, I was pulled up short by the phrase "his incomparably great power for us who believe." Quick question. What do you plan to do with that power?

I'm thinking about Dodge trucks with the HEMI power system, which seems to give a lot of power to the otherwise regular guys who are lucky enough to acquire one . . . at least on the commercials. "That thing got a HEMI?" the driver is asked. Then come the looks of awe and admiration as he sits a bit taller and smiles smugly.

Why is it that we don't zero in with huge curiosity on the availability and the extent of the power Paul says is ours in Christ? I'm not talking willpower, the power to be good, or some superior, self-righteous attitude where we look down on the wretched refuse. I'm talking about the power that gave Jesus back His life . . . that made the sea calm down and the fish show up . . . that made blind folks see and deaf guys hear. Check out John 14:12, where Jesus says that anyone who has faith in Him will do greater things than the miracles the disciples had seen. So, I believe! So what do I do with information like this?

Two weeks and five days ago I was praying for a desperately ill friend and the crazy thought came to me: "Get off your couch, grab the oil, and go to the hospital." It was so hard for me to obey. But the thought was gigantic and wouldn't go away. So I went.

As I drove, I was increasingly anxious . . . afraid maybe? Finally I found my friend, told her and her husband about my prayers, anointed her forehead with oil in the name of Jesus and prayed with some sort of authority. HEMI! She didn't think I was stupid; neither did her husband.

Once I had obeyed, the whole atmosphere changed. The feeling of being a fool was gone. In the car on the way home my mind filled with a sense of authority . . . of power . . . and I began to speak out loud the names of people who were on my mind—five names, over and over. It was as if the mention of each name was a brick in a wall of protection surrounding them.

Here's the deal. My friend is fine. Her doctor said things abruptly changed that afternoon. The other names on the list *all* surfaced on my phone or e-mail—two with cancer stories, one with a liver ailment, and my own sweet brother who is struggling with a lung disease. Each was prompted to contact me (one from Baghdad!). Coincidence? I don't think so. Goosebumps, guys. Goosebumps!

What would happen if we took the power that is ours seriously? People who make a big deal about it . . . well, I'll reserve my reaction to that. But to go about quietly using God's power, even if you look like a fool, that's something else.

We need to tell each other when Jesus does something through us—without being arrogant, or smiling smugly like the HEMI guy. Otherwise we only remember the religious arguments and emotions, not the real power and the Source of that power.

Jesus said: "*All* authority in heaven and on earth has been given to me. Therefore go . . . " (Matthew 28:18ff, emphasis added). Think about it.

> "I pray also that the eyes of your heart may be enlightened in order that you may know the hope to which he has called you, the riches of his glorious inheritance in the saints, and his *incomparably great power* for us who believe." (Ephesians 1:18–19, emphasis added)

## Stuff

I stood today in the black and dripping remains of my friends' home. Last night it was struck by lightning and destroyed in the ensuing fire. Theirs was a truly lovely home—a masterpiece. Over the years they have collected just the right pieces, just the right colors, and just last week put the final touch on nine years of work—the landscaping. Today I stood in the living room, ankle-deep in wet, black gunk, looking through the wall into what used to be the bedroom and out into the backyard. Upstairs there is still a floor, a few doorframes, some burned-up beds and the melted remains of ceiling fans. No roof. As I write this I still can smell the smoke.

Recently I finished reading the biography of Amy Carmichael, and the words of her call to ministry echo in my mind: "If any man builds on this foundation [Christ] using gold, silver, costly stones, wood, hay or straw, his work will be shown for what it is, because the Day will bring it to light. It will be revealed with fire, and the fire will test the quality of each man's work. If what he has built survives, he will receive his reward. If it is burned up, he will suffer loss; he himself will be saved, but only as one escaping through the flames" (1 Corinthians 3:12–15).

Somehow these words, coupled with the strong smell of a burned-down house in my nostrils, make me weep. What am I building? Take away the stuff of this world . . . the titles and buildings, salaries and resumes . . . burn it all up, and what is left of my work? Am I truly investing my time and my life in gold, silver, and precious stones, or am I wasting my energy on wood, hay, and straw?

My dad had a plaque by his desk when I was little that I now have over mine: "Only one life, 'twill soon be past. Only what's done for Jesus Christ will last."

Do what matters. All the other stuff is just . . . other stuff.

> "For no one can lay any foundation other than the one already laid, which is Jesus Christ. If any man builds on this foundation using gold, silver, costly stones, wood, hay or straw, his work will be shown for what it is." (1 Corinthians 3:11–13)

## Near to the Heart

Tuesdays are busy for me. There are people here at the house non-stop on Tuesdays, and I am stretched a little farther than my limit. Then comes Wednesday. Ah, sweet Wednesday. What a pleasurable thing it is for me to wake up to a purposefully unscheduled day and spend time going over your names and faces with the Lord on Wednesday mornings.

This morning I have an old hymn rambling through my mind:

> There is a place of quiet rest, near to the heart of God.
> A place where sin cannot molest, near to the heart of God.
> O Jesus, blest Redeemer, sent from the heart of God,
> Hold us who wait before thee near to the heart of God.
> —Cleland B. McAfee

Nothing deep today . . . nothing thought-provoking or clever . . . just a sigh and a word of wisdom from one of the oldest children you may know. Enjoy the hug today. Hear the heartbeat of God and smile deep down as you remember that you are His twice. Once because He made you and once because He bought you back after you got lost.

Going to that place, even for just a little while, can set the tone for the whole day. Remember.

"I will put my trust in him." (Hebrews 2:13)

## Room for You

This morning it's just me and the dogs here, so I took the time to fix a little breakfast, set the table, and light the candles. I love candles. For me, they are a good visible reminder of the Light— the presence of the Spirit of God. I love to have a candle burning when I open God's Word or pray. (It gives me something to look at that isn't distracting.) Anyhow, it was a sweet time of mentioning your name and listening to what God might have to say for this day.

Think about a time when you've met someone for dinner, or when you've run into friends in a restaurant and they've made room for you at their table. Nice, isn't it? Then there are other times when you run into people who are already in a group, and while they are cordial, they let you know by their conversation or their actions that their group is formed and you aren't a part of it. That hurts.

As I sat at the table today, thinking of you and talking to the Father, it hit me hard enough to bring tears—there is room at His table for me . . . and for you. In the place where God's company and His nourishment can be enjoyed, there is always a place for you and a place for me.

That's enough for me.

> "'Here I am! I stand at the door and knock. If anyone hears my voice and opens the door, I will come in and eat with him, and he with me.'" (Revelation 3:20)

## Grace to You (Grace and the Passion of Christ)

The words of a song I recently learned are tumbling over themselves in my head. "Grace to you . . . may grace abound in all you do. Grace to do the will of the Father." Ah, grace! A very good gift. Brings a contented smile to my face.

When Mel Gibson was interviewed by Diane Sawyer after the release of his movie *The Passion*, my husband, Jon, and I were trying to figure out her reaction. She was upset about the violence in the movie and wondered why we had to see that. She was worried about people being offended by Christ's suffering, and she was uneasy about blaming the cross on anybody.

"Who killed Jesus Christ?" she asked.

"The big answer is, we all did," said Mel Gibson. "I'll be first in the culpability stakes here, you know."

Watching her response to this and her subsequent questions, Jon looked at me and said, "She just doesn't get it." Reminds me of the same sentiment expressed by Augustine: "Unless you believe you won't understand." It also reminds me of Dietrich Bonhoeffer railing at the thought of "cheap grace."

I pray for us today . . . that we will each take time to ponder the cost of grace. And at the risk of being a bit over the top, let me bring you a word from one other saint as she pondered this cost:

> Surely, O Lord, the fearful death that awaited you on earth must have been for you a source of great pain and sorrow? "No," you reply; "such pain is readily transcended by the great love that I have for you and my longing that your souls might be saved. Since I left this earth I have suffered and continue to suffer to such a degree that by comparison the former pain does not merit the least consideration."
>
> —Saint Teresa of Avila (*Interior Castle*)

It is finished . . . the price paid . . . and yet people just don't get it. Until I read this, I hadn't really thought about the on-going suffering of Jesus as He intercedes for all of His beloved who just don't get it. Drives me to find time today to thank Him, and to yell: "I GET IT!"

God's free grace. Enormously costly. Incredibly sweet!

Grace to each of us today.

> "And the God of all grace, who called you to his eternal glory in Christ, after you have suffered a little while, will himself restore you and make you strong, firm and steadfast. To him be the power for ever and ever. Amen." (1 Peter 5:10–11)

## Flies!

A friend of mine told me this story.

Once there was a man who noticed a fly in his kitchen. He chased it down with a fly swatter and, after only a few minutes, killed it. It wasn't long before he noticed another fly. This one he got with a snap of a dishtowel. As he tried to find food for lunch, he kept noticing more and more flies, but he went after each of them and prevailed.

A friend, hoping to share lunch with the man, arrived at his house and took a seat in the kitchen. He watched as the man hunted and killed flies until he could stay silent no longer. "My friend, what are you doing?" he asked.

"See how well I can control the flies in my kitchen" the man replied with pride.

"That's good," answered his friend. "But why don't you just take out the garbage?"

So here's the question for today. Are you more interested in handling the flies in your life or in getting rid of the source of the problem?

I know someone who suffered for years with an eating disorder. She kept it a secret because of the shame she felt, and controlling it occupied much of her time. But her entire focus was on controlling a harmful behavior instead of on healing. As a result, it nearly killed her. Then one day she recognized a sin that was feeding the problem. In her case, it was a failure to believe that God meant it when He said He loved her! Tearfully she took out the garbage—her controlling desire to earn the Father's love—and was astonished to find freedom from handling the flies!

We each have our own garbage. Ignoring it means that we will be spending the majority of our energy fighting flies.

Take a critical look at the things that require too much of your energy. Then take out the garbage.

"If we claim to be without sin, we deceive ourselves and the truth is not in us. If we confess our sins, he is faithful and just and will forgive us our sins and purify us from all unrighteousness. If we claim we have not sinned, we make him out to be a liar and his word has no place in our lives." (1 John 1:8–10)

## On the Tip of Your Mind

"Imagination is the greatest gift God has given us and it ought to be devoted entirely to Him."
—Oswald Chambers

I don't know what you're going to face today or this week, but I want you to remember that there was a time when Jesus faced a similar thing. There isn't a thing you will suffer or a thing that will tempt you that Jesus hasn't faced, on an actual day and time, as He lived His life here on earth.

Remembering this and using God's gifts of His Word and your imagination can allow you to seek Him and find Him and understand that He faced what you are facing. What caused His struggle? How did He handle it? Bring your situation to Him and ask Him questions about your struggles. He's your instant role model and your source of help and strength . . . right on the tip of your mind . . . if you remember to go there.

Think about it. If there is no joy or pain that is unique to us (as it says in Hebrews 4), then whatever we face in a day, Jesus has faced, and faced it successfully. If we are to become like Christ, shouldn't our reactions be like His?

We have more than God's Word as a rule to live by; we actually have His presence to live with us. So often we are consumed with doing the right things and acting the right ways that we forget that first and foremost we have His promise to be with us, no matter what circumstances we face.

He's right there—on the tip of your mind.

> "For we do not have a high priest who is unable to sympathize with our weaknesses, but we have one who has been tempted in every way, just as we are—yet was without sin. Let us then approach the throne of grace with confidence, so that we may receive mercy and find grace to help us in our time of need." (Hebrews 4:15–16)

## Walk on Your Knees

I am reading today about Jesus washing His disciples' feet. Washing somebody else's dirty feet is a nasty thing. Actually, just caring for dirty people is a nasty thing. Yet Jesus did this everyday, necessary chore (imagine how dirty those sandal-clad feet got in that dusty land) in such a way that I can no longer hear the words "foot-washing" without seeing a mental picture of Him making it an amazingly beautiful act of love. Foot-washing has become something reverent and holy.

So, I look at my list of chores for the day . . . laundry, cleaning, writing, being with people who have needs . . . and I wonder how these ordinary things can become acts of love, reverent and holy. Is it possible? When I look at the people and the work I face today . . . the everyday, unimpressive, common and maybe even nasty . . . can there be anything beautiful or holy there? Wouldn't it be grand to have a mental picture of Jesus doing what I need to do today? Honestly, how would He do what I need to do? Would He do all of the things on my list? Did He really mean to ask me to follow His example in everyday chores and interactions with people? (I notice that even Judas got his feet washed.)

The power of God in the flesh was that His touch could make everyday, ordinary, nasty chores into something reverent and holy. The power of God in you and me can do exactly that, too. Today I will be praying for your desire to wash feet.

Somehow "walk well" doesn't cover it today. See if you can walk on your knees.

Read John 13:1–17.

> "'I have set you an example that you should do as I have done for you. I tell you the truth, no servant is greater than his master, nor is a messenger greater than the one who sent him. Now that you know these things, you will be blessed if you do them.'" (John 13:15–17)

## Stand by Me

The promise of God's leading is something we count on, and the anticipation of seeing Him use us is our inspiration to keep going. Those of us who have allowed God to take us into crazy circumstances of faith and who have been amazed to realize that God Almighty really does take pleasure in using ordinary people, find ourselves looking for the next opportunity to be obedient . . . the next chance to be a part of what God is doing. A walk of faith can be an extraordinarily breathtaking experience.

But for some of us the walk of faith has resulted in bruises that have yet to heal. People and circumstances aren't always kind to us as we seek to be faithful. A deep exhaustion sometimes leaves believers conflicted between their desire to experience more of the life God has for them and the need to pull back into a time of rest where they can recoup, heal, and get a second wind. Bounding on in hope and dragging on in borrowed strength . . . exhilaration and agony struggling together to form our next step. This is the reality of the Christian walk.

My prayer for you each today is that you get taken by surprise with the joy of remembering that you have been called . . . chosen . . . to speak Jesus' word to a world filled with bored people who don't believe in miracles. May His reality, His peace, and His enthusiasm take you over. And when you wonder if you have the strength to take on this walk for another day, let me encourage you with these words that my son sent to me.

> In the midst of tribulations, stand by me;
> In the midst of tribulations, stand by me;
> When the hosts of hell assail,
> And my strength begins to fail;
> Thou who never lost a battle, stand by me.
> —Charles Tindley ("Stand by Me," 1905)

"Thou who never lost a battle, stand by me." Gotta love that!

> "But as surely as God is faithful, our message to you is not 'Yes' and 'No.' For the Son of God, Jesus Christ, who was preached among you by me and Silas and Timothy, was not 'Yes' and 'No,' but in him it has always been 'Yes.' For no matter how many promises God has made, they are 'Yes' in Christ. . . . Now it is God who makes both us and you stand firm in Christ." (2 Corinthians 1:18–21)

## Struggle Is Not Failure

I used to think that struggle was a sign that someone was losing a battle with wrong choices. I grew up putting on a strong, happy face and just wading through difficulties quietly. I thought that was how strong folks did things. They knew the right answers and made the right decisions . . . no problem.

Today I am wiser. Today I can't hide the fact that much of life is a struggle.

I struggle with God's calling on my life and His demands on my heart. I struggle with my need to accomplish and God's call to relinquish. I read an amazing thing by Oswald Chambers this week: "It is easier to serve God without a vision, easier to work for God without a call, because then you are not bothered by what God requires; common sense is your guide, veneered over with Christian sentiment." God's call and God's vision *will* produce struggle. There are always people who have a better idea . . . who might not understand or embrace the vision that God has given. But keep on. Be true. Your obedience becomes what God most requires and desires of you. Keep on.

I wonder if you struggle with the opinions of others who don't understand your call or your vision. I wonder if you deal with wonderful people who have grand ideas and talents and ambitions, but who just don't understand that sometimes God actually leads us in ways that don't make us look successful. Sometimes God asks us to stand firm against popular opinion . . . sometimes even against our friends. That kind of struggle is not a sign of weakness, but of overcoming strength.

Keep struggling to be true to your call. Even if the cost is high. As I read the story of Jesus in the garden of Gethsemane right

206

before He was arrested, I notice struggle. That's what makes the victory so remarkable and huge. Struggle isn't failure. In fact, when there is no struggle, I wonder about the call.

You are lifted up today with this ferocious plea: God, help us to keep struggling to be true to the call we have heard from you. Guard us from distractions and from the need to accomplish. Help us to seek your nod of approval above even the love or respect of those we love. Struggle doesn't come because you disapprove of us. Encourage us to remember that obedience is the point.

> "But you, man of God, flee from all this, and pursue righteousness, godliness, faith, love, endurance and gentleness. Fight the good fight of the faith. Take hold of the eternal life to which you were called when you made your good confession in the presence of many witnesses. . . . Guard what has been entrusted to your care. Turn away from godless chatter and the opposing ideas of what is falsely called knowledge, which some have professed and in so doing have wandered from the faith." (1 Timothy 6:11-12, 20–21)

## Lingering

The room that is now my office used to be my son's bedroom. Mostly it's filled with my stuff now, but there are still a few stickers on the door and books on the shelves that are his. It's a little cold today, so I opened the closet and got out one of the shirts hanging there to keep me warm. As I write this, my mind is filled with Kevin because this shirt smells like him. Not any particular smell . . . like after-shave or anything . . . just a subtle smell that no one but his mom would probably notice. It's almost like this shirt is hugging me.

Psychologists say that smells are some of the strongest memory triggers in the brain. So here's a thought. What does God smell like? In 2 Corinthians 2:14–16 Paul talks about "the aroma of Christ." What exactly is the aroma of Christ? Paul says, "Thanks be to God, who always leads us in triumphal procession in Christ and through us spreads everywhere the fragrance of the knowledge of him" (2 Corinthians 2:14).

Paul is writing to people who are familiar with triumphal processions of Roman governors, where soldiers and captives would march through town while people cheered and burned sweet-smelling spices in the streets. So he seems to be saying that Christians are to give off an aroma, a fragrance that should remind the world of Christ.

What about your life would remind someone of Jesus? Is it possible that proximity to you could make someone feel hugged by Him? Not because of what you say necessarily, but because of the aroma of His character in you. Imagine someone saying to you, "You remind me of Jesus."

My prayer for you this morning is that something sweet will linger after you've gone. That someone will indeed think, "You remind me of Jesus."

"For we are to God the aroma of Christ among those who are being saved and those who are perishing." (2 Corinthians 2:15)

## In Your Face, Peace

"The Lord bless you and keep you; the Lord make his face
shine upon you and be gracious to you; the Lord turn his
face toward you and give you peace." (Numbers 6:24–26).

That's my prayer for you this morning. God told Moses to bless
his group with this blessing (they were rather prone to worry, you
know). Basically it says,

"Today God wants only the best for you. Look into His face and
you will see that He is absolutely pleased with you! Look into His
eyes and let Him make everything all right."

Breathe in the reality of the God who is as near to you as the air
you breathe. Set aside your "ought to's" and your "shoulds"—just
set them all aside and look into the kindest, most loving face,
which is totally loving you.

Now, just rest there for a few minutes and ask Him to stay like
that all day . . . right in your face.

"As a father has compassion on his children, so the Lord
has compassion on those who fear him." (Psalm 103:13)

## Awe

I just walked a few miles around a nearby lake with a friend, and
I was overcome by creation. Then I came home and flipped on the

TV and saw a promo for a new show, *Joan of Arcadia*. It's about a girl who keeps running into God. The first time He tells her who He is, she asks for a miracle. He points to a tree. She says, "That's just a tree!" And He replies. "Yeah? Let's see you make one."

So today my attention is drawn to the miracles all around me that I take for granted. Like trees. I mean, what kind of mind thinks up so many kinds of trees? How is it that they produce "after their own kind" (Genesis 1) and retain such unique features? I saw two bushes today right next to each other. One had soft leaves and clusters of insanely purple berries, and the other had sticky leaves and thorns and wonderful clusters of bright orange berries. They were planted in the same dirt . . . received the same sunshine and rain . . . yet were totally different. There had to have been tens of thousands of different kinds of plants just around that one park—some poison, some healthy, some medicinal. Why? How? What makes an apple taste different from a carrot? Why do some plants smell? And what does my little mind do with a tree that has flowers one season, green leaves and fruit the next, and then the leaves burst into color and fall off . . . only to let the plant rest and get ready to do it all again? I mean, really! How does a tree turn dirt, water and sunshine into flowers and leaves?

In the beginning, at creation, God kept checking out His creation and pronouncing it good. Then He took a day off to rest (Genesis 2:2–3).

God took a day off! What do you think He did on His day off? Maybe enjoyed His creation?

God took a day off! How can I be too busy to take time off and worship the Creator by enjoying His creative genius?

True worship is noticing God and enjoying Him, and we don't spend nearly enough time in awe of creation. Today, take time— and let the magnificence of a leaf or a flower overcome you. Take time—just order yourself a mixed greens and veggie salad somewhere and try to wrap your mind around the fact that man just can't make that stuff!

Walk with your eyes wide open today. Notice things. Remember God.

> "By the seventh day God had finished the work he had been doing; so on the seventh day he rested from all his work. And God blessed the seventh day and made it holy, because on it he rested from all the work of creating that he had done." (Genesis 2:2–3)

## Toys and Tools

I've been up in the attic pulling out Christmas stuff, and I noticed that my attic is full of toys. I've got bristle blocks and Legos, blocks of wood and construx sets—toys that were really wonderful to play with when my kids were learning to build things and put things together. My attic also has a place where the wood needs to be replaced on the house. Those toys were a good way to learn about building, but they won't be of any help at all in actually repairing a real house. Only a fool would think that children's toys would be adequate for maintaining a home. I need to get some real lumber and nails to solve that problem.

It's all about learning, isn't it? I remember my childlike understanding of the baby in the manger. I remember seeing a manger scene in our neighborhood—complete with Santa, Rudolph, and Frosty—and being mesmerized by the camels and sheep and that shiny star. That was enough to begin teaching me the basics of building faith when I was little. But as I've grown up,

I've needed to move beyond that to the reality of the entire story of salvation.

Why is it that Christianity is so hollow and meaningless for so many people? Could it be that they have settled for the religious "toys" of their childhood . . . which aren't bad, but were never meant to sustain real, adult life? Have you actually used the tools of faith? Actually involved God in the problems and maintenance of your life? It takes effort and practice and learning to move from toys to tools.

It's interesting how people who would never think of using children's toys to do their accounting or marketing or for the running of their homes or their businesses are perfectly content to run their spiritual lives with nothing more than a few holiday characters, carols, and traditions. Be smarter than that. Get started in learning how to use heavy spiritual machinery.

If the whole world is focused on the birth of Christ, shouldn't that include learning about who He is and what He's been up to since He was born in Bethlehem? There's a bunch more good news and power involved here than most folks think!

God coming to earth . . . this is not child's play. This is the serious stuff of life.

> "When I was a child, I talked like a child, I thought like a child, I reasoned like a child. When I became a man, I put childish ways behind me. Now we see but a poor reflection as in a mirror; then we shall see face to face. Now I know in part; then I shall know fully, even as I am fully known."
> (1 Corinthians 13:11–12)

212

## December Peace Fix

I've been hauling boxes out of the attic and wrapping things in holly and red bows. Tiny bundles carefully wrapped in tissue hold treasures made by my kids another lifetime ago. I'm unpacking and setting out lots of old, old stuff with no street value at all, and yet the lights on the tree and the little wooden people standing about on coffee tables and windowsills bring something familiar and safe to our home. It's the memory of Christmases past. It's traditions that go back to my parents and their parents and so on, back into the past. Traditions. Things that don't change. Things that pass on story and meaning and memories—and bring peace and calm in the midst of what can be a very busy, even hectic, time of year.

The advertising world would have us believe that anything good needs to be new, improved, bigger, faster, louder. And yet that's not what I'm hoping to find this Advent season. As we wait for the arrival—"arrival" is what advent means—of Christmas and our remembrance of Jesus' birth, I want peace and quiet to surround my thoughts and my days. I hope I can make my home a place like that. Not peace and quiet that says "I'm bored with nothing to do," but peace and quiet that means calm and joy even when there are tons of things to do.

Perhaps the words of the angels who came to announce the birth of Jesus on that first Christmas will help us remember God's intent for that night.

> "'Glory to God in the highest, and on earth peace to men on whom his favor rests.'" (Luke 2:14)

## Take It Captive

The trees are hanging on to the snow that God dumped on them last night like they know how beautiful it makes them. When I got up this morning the world was fresh and white. Blue sky . . . sunshine . . . and clean white snow. The wonderful thing about all this is that I feel the same way inside. Clean and fresh. Of all God's gifts to us, I think the fresh start He gives us is the most precious. I'm really aware of that this morning, because my day didn't start out this way . . .

I awoke from a bad dream at about 5:00 A.M. and just lay there and thought about it. The dream was so real, and for a few minutes in the darkness I let my mind retrace memories I have long since asked God to free me from—unpleasant things, hurtful things. Before I realized it, I was working up a pretty dismal mood . . . my whole body felt sad. So I went to God and asked Him, "Take this away!" Then I lay there for a little while longer and ruminated in the sludge of my dream until once again I prayed, "God, take this all away!" I got up early, dragged my heavy heart to the kitchen for some coffee, and settled down for a little time of prayer and quiet. "God! Why are these thoughts back? Why won't you take them away?"

I opened my daily devotions book and read the words of Oswald Chambers: "God does not give us overcoming life; He gives us life *as we overcome*." BAM! *Why in the world am I asking God to do something I have the power to change?* I wondered. I will take my thoughts another place and deny the enemy the pleasure of seeing me derail this morning. I am not the victim of a memory or a dream. I am God's kid, and He will give me the strength to act like it! Then I prayed, "God, I will not let go of the life you pour in as I overcome! This bad dream is over. Fill me up to face this day. Lift the weight. Erase guilt that is not mine. Remind me of who I am."

And the peace of God that passes understanding rushed into my morning like warm water being drawn for a bath. I looked out the window and noticed the beauty, stroked my dog's head, and found a defiant smile had taken over my face. That's how days need to begin: confession, acknowledging the need for God's power, crying out for a clean start, and then getting busy to make it happen. Satan leaves . . . running . . . when God is invited in. God will give me everything I need to get the job done, and then give me life—overcoming life—as I begin to work in the power He provides.

Get into the habit of *running* to God each morning and asking for a fresh start. Don't carry yesterday's hurts and wounds into a fresh new day.

Before you dwell on the thoughts that come to your mind today, look them over, edit them, and accept only the ones that lead to life. Use the power God provides to bring your thoughts under His control. Overcome.

> "We demolish arguments and every pretension that sets itself up against the knowledge of God, and we take captive every thought to make it obedient to Christ."
> (2 Corinthians 10:5)

## Amazing Love

Every so often reality breaks through my thoughts and I am faced, as if for the first time, with a truth I have long accepted, but which has become common to me. How is it that the majesty and awe of God Almighty can become commonplace? How is it that I can bow my head for a quick grace before a meal, or rush through a time of prayer without being hit afresh with the holiness of God? I know I am to enter His throne room with confidence and to think of Him as my father . . . even more, my Abba Father . . . and yet, is it possible that I don't feel the white-hot heat of His glory anymore? How can I casually look for Him in my day, when somewhere deep inside I know that no one can see Him and live? Where is the trembling? Where is the holy fear? How can I find words to prattle on when I am in the presence of the Word Himself?

This morning I sit in awe. Eyes wet. Mouth gaping but silent.

Awe is a thing we need to feel every day. A sense of the inexplicability of God Almighty that takes not only my words but my breath away.

This day my mind fills with the words Charles Wesley penned over 250 years ago in the awe-filled presence of Jesus. Imagine the shaking hand and the tear-bleary eyes that wrote these lyrics in a moment of, "O my God!" awe. Read these words and take them personally . . .

> He left His Father's throne above,
> So free, so infinite His grace!
> Emptied Himself of all but love,
> And bled for Adam's helpless race!
> 'Tis mercy all, immense and free,
> For *O my God, it found out me.*
>
> Amazing love! How can it be
> That thou, my God, shouldst die for me!

> "Therefore, there is now no condemnation for those who are in Christ Jesus . . . .The Spirit himself testifies with our spirit that we are God's children. Now if we are children, then we are heirs—heirs of God and co-heirs with Christ, if indeed we share in his sufferings in order that we may also share in his glory." (Romans 8:1, 16–17)

## Swedish Ivy (1)

Today is pruning day, and I just spent an hour or so cutting back my Swedish Ivy. It is the most beautiful plant I've ever had, and my inclination is just to let it keep growing, especially since the new leaves are the prettiest green. But I know that if I don't cut it back, it will get spindly and stalky, and come fall, it won't be healthy enough to yield its flowers. It will need to get cut back eventually, either totally to the stump, because it has grown unchecked and become unhealthy, or gradually so that it will stay healthy.

But pruning isn't just for plants. Jesus gives us a spiritual pruning lesson in John 15:1–2. "I am the true vine, and my Father is the gardener," He says. "He cuts off every branch in me that bears no fruit, while every branch that does bear fruit he prunes so that it will be even more fruitful."

We all have dead branches that need to be chopped off (bad habits, wrong priorities, bad attitudes), but here's what captured my attention today. Sometimes things that seem to be bearing fruit need to be pruned so that they will be even more fruitful.

What do I mean by that? Well, I believe in my own life it means that I need to tend to my own spiritual health and seek to live sensibly. Being too busy, exhausting my resources may be producing pretty new leaves, but is it more leaves than fruit? Am I getting spindly and stalky—stretched a bit too thin, and far from my root? I believe Jesus is saying that even some beautiful leaves may need to go so that I can grow into a branch healthy enough to bear the fruit He has in mind.

Too often we tend to judge our spiritual health by our pretty leaves (busyness, praise from others, number of church-related activities, reading the right books, listening to the right music) more than our fruit (Galatians 5:22–23). Our primary concern needs to be our own health as a branch connected to the Vine and the evidence of His fruit, not just a lot of pretty leaves. Only healthy, pruned branches bear good fruit that is pleasing to the Gardener.

Sometimes the most unselfish thing you can do is say no to things that bear more leaves than fruit in your own life.

> "But the fruit of the Spirit is love, joy, peace, patience, kindness, goodness, faithfulness, gentleness and self-control." (Galatians 5:22–23)

## Swedish Ivy (2)

So, I lopped off great pieces of Swedish Ivy and now the plant looks healthier. But what do I do with all the fallen branches? Well, guess what! The healthy branches that have been pruned hold amazing potential. If I handle them right, I should end up with several more Swedish Ivy plants. I need to trim away excess leaves and place the stems into a nurturing environment that will encourage the development of roots—that is, put them in water and sunlight. The goal, of course, is to develop a root system that can support a healthy plant that can thrive apart from the original.

When you do some pruning in your life (and in your schedule), certain good and valuable things may need to be taken away. Maybe someone else needs to lead your small group, or teach your class for a while. That doesn't mean those things are no longer viable and valuable. How often I hear of people trapped by their

218

own excellence in ministry and their love and devotion for the programs to which they give themselves. "If I stop, the program will die!" Pruning is not about killing something; it's about establishing new plants/new growth.

Think of Timothy and Paul. Paul's ministry in Ephesus was effective. But when it was time for him to move on, he pruned the Ephesus branch from his responsibilities and made sure it would propagate properly under Timothy's leadership. Paul invested his life in Timothy, not so that he could be a great assistant, but so that he could thrive on his own and carry on the work.

I've heard it said, "Without a successor there is no success." Well, amen to that. Take a look at the contributions you make to your church, to your ministry. Are you taking the time to raise up and mentor a successor who will keep the work going when it is time for you to move on?

Who will continue the work when you are done?

> "'Therefore go and make disciples of all nations, baptizing them in the name of the Father and of the Son and of the Holy Spirit, and teaching them to obey everything I have commanded you. And surely I am with you always, to the very end of the age.'" (Matthew 28:19–20)

## Benediction

I wonder sometimes why God has put certain people on my heart. I wonder sometimes about the value of spending so much time in prayer and listening. This morning I have stumbled upon a good answer to my questions in the writings of Henri Nouwen.

He says that blessings are not just random good things that happen to us but rather are *words* of truth and affirmation spoken into our lives. "Blessing" comes from the Latin word *benedicere*, which means speaking (*dicto*) well (*bene*) about someone. It's also where we get the word *benediction*.

> The problem of modern living is that we are too busy—looking for affirmation in the wrong places—to notice that we are being blessed. Often, people say good things about us, but we brush them aside with remarks such as, "Oh, don't mention it, forget about it, it was nothing . . . " and so on. These remarks may seem to be expressions of true humility, but they are, in fact, signs that we are not truly present to receive the blessings that are given. It is not easy for us, busy people, to truly receive a blessing. Perhaps the fact that few people offer a real blessing is the sad result of the absence of people who are willing and able to receive such a blessing. It has become extremely difficult for us to stop, listen, pay attention and receive gracefully what is offered to us. (*Becoming the Beloved*)

Blessings are not the same thing as luck. Blessings come in the power of a word of truth, commissioned by God, for the intentional purpose of our encouragement.

Now I know why He reminds me of you and why each of your names needs to be spoken in prayer and why each of you needs to hear an occasional benediction. The truth about you is that you are God's beloved, and it is important to Him that you are encouraged.

This week be aware of blessings . . . words of truth . . . intended for you to actually hear and accept, and don't turn even one away. Receive them gracefully.

> "I always thank God for you because of his grace given you in Christ Jesus. For in him you have been enriched in every way—in all your speaking and in all your knowledge—because our testimony about Christ was

confirmed in you. Therefore you do not lack any spiritual gift as you eagerly wait for our Lord Jesus Christ to be revealed. He will keep you strong to the end, so that you will be blameless on the day of our Lord Jesus Christ. God, who has called you into fellowship with his Son Jesus Christ our Lord, is faithful." (1 Corinthians 1:4–9)

# RECOMMENDED BOOKS ON PRAYER

The following books either teach or demonstrate the richness of a life of prayer:

Baillie, John. *A Diary of Private Prayer*. New York: Simon and Schuster, 1996.

Boa, Kenneth. *Face to Face: Praying the Scriptures*. Grand Rapids, Mich.: Zondervan, 1997.

Bounds, *E. M. Bounds on Prayer*. New Kensington, Pa.: Whitaker House, 1997.

Capalbo, Battistina, comp. *Praying with Saint Teresa*. Grand Rapids, Mich.: Eerdmans, 1997.

Carmichael, Amy. *If*. Fort Washington, Pa.: Christian Literature Crusade, 1992.

Chambers, Oswald. *My Utmost for His Highest*. Grand Rapids, Mich.: Discovery House, 1992.

Christenson, Evelyn. *What Happens When Women Pray?* Colorado Springs: Victor Books, 1992.

Dawson, John. *Taking Our Cities for God*. Lake Mary, Fla.: Creation House, 1989.

*Foster, Richard. *Prayer: Finding the Heart's True Home*. San Francisco: Harper, 1992.

Hallesby, O. *Prayer*. Minneapolis: Augsburg Fortress, 1994.

Manning, Brennan. *Abba's Child*. Colorado Springs: NavPress, 1994.

Murray, Andrew. *With Christ in the School of Prayer*. Grand Rapids, Mich.: Zondervan, 1983.

Nouwen, Henri J. M. *In the Name of Jesus*. New York: Crossroad, 1989.

Underhill, Evelyn. *Concerning the Inner Life*. New York: Penguin Putnam, 1995.

*Most highly recommended.

# NOTE TO THE READER

The publisher invites you to share your response to the message of this book by writing Discovery House Publishers, P.O. Box 3566, Grand Rapids, MI 49501, U.S.A. For information about other Discovery House books, music, videos, or DVDs, contact us at the same address or call 1-800-653-8333. Find us on the Internet at http://www.dhp.org/ or send e-mail to books@dhp.org.